Amplifying Your Effectiveness

COLLECTED ESSAYS

Also Available from DORSET HOUSE

*Adaptive Software Development: A Collaborative Approach to
Managing Complex Systems*
by James A. Highsmith III
ISBN: 0-932633-40-4   Copyright ©2000   392 pages, softcover

Exploring Requirements: Quality Before Design
by Donald C. Gause and Gerald M. Weinberg
ISBN: 0-932633-13-7   Copyright ©1989   320 pages, hardcover

Peopleware: Productive Projects and Teams, 2nd ed.
by Tom DeMarco and Timothy Lister
ISBN: 0-932633-43-9   Copyright ©1999   264 pages, softcover

Project Retrospectives: A Handbook for Team Reviews
by Norm Kerth
ISBN: 0-932633-44-7   Copyright ©2000   est. 240 pages, softcover

The Psychology of Computer Programming: Silver Anniversary Edition
by Gerald M. Weinberg
ISBN: 0-932633-42-0   Copyright ©1998   360 pages, softcover

Quality Software Management Series   by Gerald M. Weinberg

> *Vol. 1: Systems Thinking*
> ISBN: 0-932633-22-6   Copyright ©1992   336 pages, hardcover

> *Vol. 2: First-Order Measurement*
> ISBN: 0-932633-24-2   Copyright ©1993   360 pages, hardcover

> *Vol. 3: Congruent Action*
> ISBN: 0-932633-28-5   Copyright ©1994   328 pages, hardcover

> *Vol. 4: Anticipating Change*
> ISBN: 0-932633-32-3   Copyright ©1997   504 pages, hardcover

Shaping Projects: A Roundtable on Best Practices
edited by James Bullock, Gerald M. Weinberg, and Marie Benesh
ISBN: 0-932633-48-X   Copyright ©2000   est. 200 pages, softcover

Find Out More about These and Other DH Books:

Contact us to request a Book & Video Catalog and a free issue of *The
Dorset House Quarterly,* or to confirm price and shipping information.

DORSET HOUSE PUBLISHING CO., INC.
353 West 12th Street   New York, NY 10014   USA
1-800-DH-BOOKS   (1-800-342-6657)   212-620-4053   fax: 212-727-1044
info@dorsethouse.com   http://www.dorsethouse.com

Amplifying Your Effectiveness

COLLECTED ESSAYS

EDITED BY
GERALD M. WEINBERG
JAMES BACH & NAOMI KARTEN

DORSET HOUSE PUBLISHING
353 WEST 12TH STREET
NEW YORK, NEW YORK 10014

Library of Congress Cataloging-in-Publication Data

Amplifying your effectiveness : collected essays / edited by Gerald M.Weinberg, James Bach, and Naomi Karten.
   p. cm.
   Includes bibliographical references and index.
   ISBN 0-932633-47-1 (softcover)
   1. Software engineering. I. Weinberg, Gerald M. II. Bach, James. III. Karten, Naomi.

   QA76.758 .A48 2000
   005.1--dc21

                                          00-059642

All product and service names appearing herein are trademarks or registered trademarks or service marks or registered service marks of their respective owners and should be treated as such.

Cover Design: David W. McClintock
Cover Graphic: Becky Winant, Esprit Systems Consulting, Inc.
Editors Photographs: Bach photo by Dennis Brack; Karten photo by S.R. Sullivan; Weinberg photo by Dani Weinberg.

Distributed in the English language in Singapore, the Philippines, and Southeast Asia by Alkem Company (S) Pte. Ltd., Singapore; in the English language in India, Bangladesh, Sri Lanka, Nepal, and Mauritius by Prism Books Pvt., Ltd., Bangalore, India; and in the English language in Japan by Toppan Co., Ltd., Tokyo, Japan.

Printed in the United States of America

Library of Congress Catalog Number: 00-059642

ISBN: 0-932633-47-1   12 11 10 9 8 7 6 5 4 3 2 1

To the participants at our
Amplifying Your Effectiveness Conference

Contents

Contents

Contents

Acknowledgments

We owe a huge thank you to all of you who encouraged and supported us as we planned our first Amplifying Your Effectiveness Conference. Your optimism, enthusiasm, and great ideas helped us turn this dream into a reality.

Permissions
Acknowledgments

pp. 9–11: Adapted by permission from James Bach, "Rethinking the Role of Testing for the e-Business Era." *Cutter IT Journal*, Vol. XIII, No. 4 (April 2000), p. 40.

pp. 21–24: Adapted by permission from Johanna Rothman, "The Perils of Parallel Projects." *Reflections*, Vol. 2, No. 1 (1999), p. 4.

pp. 54–56: Adapted by permission from Naomi Karten, "We All Surf the Web Surreptitiously." *Perceptions & Realities*, Vol. 5, No. 2 (1999), p. 3.

pp. 57–62: Adapted by permission from Gerald M. Weinberg, "Congruent Interviewing by Audition." *Contract Professional*, Vol. 4, No. 7 (March 2000), pp. 64–65.

pp. 68–70: Adapted by permission from Naomi Karten, "Life as a Lesser Flamingo." *Perceptions & Realities*, Vol. 4, No. 2 (1999), p. 3.

pp. 73–74: Adapted by permission from Richard Brenner, "Ten Project Haiku." *In-the-SPIN: Newsletter of the Boston SPIN*, Issue 29 (September 1999), pp. 1–2.

pp. 75–77: Adapted by permission from Johanna Rothman, "It's Just the First Slip." *Reflections,* Vol. 2, No. 2 (1999), p. 4.

pp. 78–81: Material adapted by permission from "Quality Begins at Home" by Brian Pioreck, published in *VB Tech Journal* (September 1996), p. 55. Copyright © 1996 by PennWell Corporation. All rights reserved.

pp. 82–87: Adapted by permission from Marie A. Benesh, "Managing Your ERP: How to Avoid Common Pitfalls of Implementation." *Software Testing & Quality Engineering,* Vol. 1, Issue 4 (July/August 1999), pp. 38–43.

pp. 95–102: Adapted by permission from Steven M. Smith, "The Satir Change Model." Original version appeared on the Web at http://www.geraldmweinberg.com/Essays (June 1998). Copyright © 1998 by Steven M. Smith.

pp. 103–13: Adapted by permission from Esther Derby, "Modeling Organizational Change." *Software Testing & Quality Engineering,* Vol. 1, Issue 6 (November/December 1999), pp. 54–58.

pp. 114–22: Adapted by permission from Patricia A. Medvick, "How to Create a Process for Development of Useful Scientific Software." Copyright © 2000 by Patricia A. Medvick. The original paper was work performed under the auspices of the U.S. Department of Energy. Reprinted by permission.

pp. 123–31: Adapted by permission from James Bach, "Good Practice Hunting." *Cutter IT Journal,* Vol. XII, No. 2 (February 1999), p. 8.

Introduction:
The Book and the
Conference

Gerald M. Weinberg

The idea for this collection of essays, *Amplifying Your Effectiveness,* arose out of a brainstorming session for a conference of the same name. A group of successful consultants and I were talking about what we didn't like about many conferences, and soon the idea for one of our own design—and for an accompanying book—was born. In our conversation, we concluded that many conferences suffer from the conference management's need to make a lot of money, the academics' need to satisfy publication requirements, and the universe's need for inertia. Since we are neither conference managers nor academics, and since we are all change artists who specialize in overcoming inertia, we decided to create our own conference. Its structure would be dictated by the needs of a different group—the attendees.

We polled ourselves to find out what we all wanted when we were the conference attendees, and we learned that we all wanted the same thing—to amplify our effectiveness—so that's what we named our conference: Amplifying Your Effectiveness (AYE). We wanted this conference to feel special to the atten-

1

dees, so we examined various traditional practices with an eye toward finding a better way.

One of the conference elements we examined was the *proceedings*—a book or CD of material given to the attendees. While proceedings often contain valuable take-away notes and information, most have little or nothing to do with the important interactions that take place at a conference. Indeed, the very worst of all conferences are those in which the presenters stand at a lectern and read, word-for-word, a paper that appears in the proceedings. Since the AYE Conference is highly interactive, with emphasis on experiential training, the proceedings must be captured in different ways, live, to reflect what's actually happening.

That's why we decided to produce not a proceedings but a *pre*-cedings—a preview of the hosts of the conference and the thinking behind it. This volume presents each of the hosts of the first AYE Conference in terms of a short biography and some written work that exemplifies their styles and interests.

The papers in this volume reflect the diversity of the contributors. Some of the contributions have been published elsewhere; some are new; some are new versions of previous works. Taken together, they form a book that transcends the conference and captures a variety of approaches and perspectives that readers can take to amplify their effectiveness.

How the Book and the Conference Relate

After we reviewed the entire manuscript, something struck us: Although these essays are not directly about the contributors' sessions at the conference, the overall substance and tone of the collection remarkably reflects our view of the entire conference. You might think of this view as a two-dimensional table. One dimension relates to whose effectiveness is being amplified. The other dimension concerns how the amplification takes place.

Whose Effectiveness Is Amplified?

In any organization, improvements in effectiveness can occur at three levels: the individual, the team, and the organization as a whole, or, as we say in our consulting work, the Self, the Other, and the Context. The essays in this book address all three levels.

A clear example of effectiveness on the individual level is Don Gray's description of the tools and principles he uses to become a more effective problem-solver. Naomi Karten's essay about building strong relationships concerns the team and how it's strengthened. And Pat Medvick's paper on creating a process for scientific software development addresses the context level.

But the real world doesn't divide that neatly, and neither do our contributors' offerings. Pat's piece also focuses on the personal characteristics of scientists who lead software change—just as Don shows his own personal characteristics as a problem-solver. Naomi's essay is about teams, but also about how you, individually, can go about introducing yourself to a team. Then again, Don's contribution is also about teams—how he teams up with other people to help them solve their problems.

Rick Brenner's lovely set of "project haiku" gives poetic form to these interactions across levels. For instance, the haiku,

> I gave estimates.
> They cut all of them in half.
> Next time I'll pad them.

shows how the organization's culture affects the individual's behavior—and implies a feedback loop that destroys an organization's ability to make good estimates. Notice how this loop is easily exposed using the personal qualities that Don and Pat discuss. And when people use Naomi's suggestions about building a team whose members really communicate with one another, the loop may never be created in the first place.

3

So, in fact, most of the essays start with one level and reveal how each level affects others. In his testing piece, James Bach starts at the individual level, with the idea that the role of testing is to find problems, then moves to the project level, considering risk; finally, he winds up at the team level and how to understand the context of testing. Brian Pioreck's amusing allegory about the family breakfast shows how the same principles of good project management apply in every aspect of our lives, including our interactions with those most dear to us. And Becky Winant's descriptions of team-destroying tactics range from the individual, to the interpersonal, to the project, to the organization.

In a larger sense, all of these writings are derived from experiences at all three levels. Some of the experiences are designed learning situations, such as Naomi's method of introducing people or Jerry Weinberg's method of interviewing by audition. Some come from daily life experience, like Don Gray's consulting practice and Kevin Fjelsted's experiences with Braille devices for computer access. And most are synthesized from experiences across a broad spectrum of organizations, like Bob King's development of his role as architect; Sharon and Ken Roberts' knowledge of how to recognize a crunch project and decide whether or not to participate; Johanna Rothman's ability to extract valuable project and personal information from project schedule slips; Eileen Strider's keys for recognizing a runaway project and for preserving one's sanity as a participant; or Esther Derby's understanding of what organizations must really undergo in order to change.

How Does the Amplification Take Place?

In the second dimension of our imaginary table are three fundamental abilities that contribute to the effectiveness of a manager or any other technical leader:

1. the ability to observe what's happening and to understand the significance of your observations

2. the ability to act congruently in difficult interpersonal situations, even though you may be confused, or angry, or so afraid you want to run away and hide

3. the ability to understand complex situations so you can plan a project and then observe and act so as to keep the project going according to plan, or modify the plan

All three abilities are essential, and your least-developed one prevents you most from amplifying your effectiveness. For example, if you lack the ability to observe, you will repeatedly do the right thing at the wrong time. If you lack the ability to act congruently, you'll constantly grind on the thought that you knew what to do, but somehow didn't do it. And, if you lack the ability to understand complex situations, you'll find yourself perpetually overloaded, reacting to one surprising crisis after another.

And so, all three abilities are sampled in this collection. Several contributions focus on observation: Johanna Rothman shows you how to glean information from project slips; Kevin Fjelsted explores the difficulties of designing information portals for blind people, suggesting how the same awareness may be used for people lacking other faculties of observation; Sharon and Ken Roberts guide you through the maze of clues as a project is about to begin; Rick Brenner's haiku are small yet powerful reminders to watch for critical moments in a project's life that might otherwise go unnoticed; Jerry Weinberg coaches you through an interviewing process; and Marie Benesh's piece shows you exactly what to watch out for when installing enterprise products.

Congruent behavior is the second strong thread of the essays: Bob King shows you how to act congruently when you're trying to do architecture with real people in real situations; Eileen Strider describes how to act congruently, so as to be a center of sanity when a project runs away; Brian Pioreck's breakfast scenario shows that you can recenter yourself even when it's a family gathering that's gone astray; Johanna

Rothman provides tools for staying focused while trying to do many things at once.

The third thread is the ability to understand complex situations: Don Gray surveys the tools he uses, and Steve Smith elaborates on the usefulness of the Satir Change Model. James Bach shows us why incorporating good practices is not the simple linear exercise some pundits seem to promise, while Esther Derby expands that understanding through the use of diagramming cause-effect relationships. Bob King describes the architect's role in understanding complex systems, while James Bach describes the tester's. Becky Winant shows how each team is a complex system, and how delicate interventions are needed if the team is not to be destroyed. Similarly, Pat Medvick reveals the complexity of scientists' individuality, and how personal differences lead to different styles of project management.

Of course, many of this book's contributions show all three abilities working in concert, and that is the goal of the conference as well—to help you to amplify your effectiveness at all three levels: yourself as an individual, your team, and your entire organization. Enjoy!

Part One:
Empowering the
Individual

Although "organizational change" is a comforting executive concept, Virginia Satir, the great family therapist, was fond of reminding us that "Change happens one person at a time." There is no organizational change without individual change, no organizational effectiveness without individual effectiveness. That's why the first essays in this volume all address dimensions of individual empowerment.

For some, individual empowerment is a matter of overcoming disempowering factors—a good example is Kevin Fjelsted's description of the struggle by blind people to have decent access to computers. Another, more intimate, example is James Bach's evolution of ideas about his role as a tester: He shows how our internal models may prevent us from understanding how broad our role can be.

Sometimes, we empower ourselves by the tools we use—physical tools, like Kevin's Braille readers, or mental tools, like Don Gray's problem-solver's tool kit. Sometimes, we empower ourselves by setting priorities, so we can do the best we can under the circumstances—like Johanna Rothman's principles for coping with multiple parallel tasks.

Finally, we empower ourselves by staying out of situations that will disempower us, as Sharon and Ken Roberts describe in their essay on how to recognize crunch projects and either transform them or say "no thanks."

The Role of Testing

James Bach

Once upon a time, I was a developer. I didn't like it. Day in and day out, the pressure wore me down. I rarely felt that my work was good enough. I never felt free to take time off. If I messed up, we would blow a deadline or ship a doggy product. After that experience, being a test manager seemed like a vacation. Testing is such a vague activity compared to programming—there's lots of wiggle room. All they wanted me to do was find problems.

I used to think that the role of testing is to find problems.

Finding problems was easy, but not very satisfying in the long run. I wanted to help the product be really *good*.

I was one of many test specialists in a group of about 400 at Apple. Since our group was called Software Quality Assurance, there was earnest talk about how quality assurance (QA) was more than just testing. One of the other managers circulated a book called *Quality Without Tears*, by Philip Crosby, as a way to help us see our deeper role in product development. The book spoke of "zero defects," and I became a convert to the philosophy of bug prevention. "You can't test quality into the product" was our mantra.

I used to think that the role of testing is to assure quality.

Testers can't really *assure* quality, though. For one thing, perfect quality is an inherently unreachable goal. There are many dimensions to it, and some of them conflict. For another thing, testers don't create quality, so such a role is not really in our power to perform. Even if we think of ourselves only as quality gatekeepers, the rest of the team will tend to take a little less responsibility for quality; they'll figure QA is there to "assure" it—and to receive the brunt of blame if the product isn't good enough.

Besides, the natural instinct of many QA people is to exert control by defining processes and auditing process compliance. The problem is that such an approach slips so easily into moralizing about quality, wherein all of the trade-offs and subtleties of excellence are lost in the glare of slogans and general arguments that good quality is good and bad quality is bad. That's why it's so common for developers to perceive QA as just an annoying buzz in their ears—just another distraction, not a contribution.

In my case, I was rescued from life as a horsefly. My manager took me aside and told me a great secret: It's all about risk—not the search for perfection, but the search for something good enough. That transforms testing and quality assurance into a form of project radar, scanning for the enemy. We are in the project to find important problems fast, not just any old problem at any old pace.

This changed my thinking profoundly. I no longer focused so much on covering the product as completely as I could in my tests, but rather on understanding what parts of the product really needed to be tested and on judging the risk of unknown problems based on known problems.

Thinking about risk brings testers more into alignment with everyone else on the project. Conversations about quality become an examination of what matters, rather than a struggle over who cares about excellence and who doesn't.

I used to think that the role of testing is to analyze risk.

Risk is important, but it's also kind of an abstract concept, and a downbeat one, at that. One development manager told me he didn't like talking about risk. "It sounds so negative. Hey, we aren't insurance actuaries, we're entrepreneurs. We take risks." He had a point. Reward is really the whole point of the project, right? Can't we find a more expansive and positive view of testing?

Certainly the point of testing is to help find problems, analyze risk, and assure quality, but there is a more essential way of looking at our role: *We light the way.* Without testing, projects blunder along in the dark, tripping over obstacles and falling over cliffs. The testing process focuses light where it's needed to help developers and management know where they are, where they ought to go, and when they have arrived.

Today, I think the role of testing is to bring vital information to light in support of the grand mission of creating great products and running the business. That includes finding problems, assessing quality, analyzing risk, and in any other way helping the team to understand what's going on.

I wonder what I'll think testing is tomorrow.

A Brief History of the Accessibility of Computers by Blind People

Kevin Fjelsted

Have you ever described a picture? What words do you use? As a blind person, I have spent my life listening to descriptions of pictures.

The interesting thing is that in most cases when we describe a picture, we actually describe characteristics of the picture, such as, "There are three people in the picture" or "This is a picture of a house." Rarely when we describe a picture do we actually describe the details of the picture. This leaves much to the imagination of the person receiving the information. For example, if I tell you that a picture is of "a house," what image comes to your mind?

We've grown up with the old adage, A picture is worth a thousand words. Even if that's true, the reality is that we do not perceive a thousand words but rather the concepts described in the picture. Clearly, whether the picture enters our imagination through a third-party description, or directly through our eyes, a massive amount of activity in the brain occurs.

In the 1950's, when the primary means of communications for computing machines was via punch cards using Hollerith codes, some blind people got very adept at debugging programs and sequences by feeling the position of the punch holes. Sighted people decoded the cards with their eyes, using the numbered guides present on the card to denote the columns and positions. With the advent of the line printer, various computer programs were developed that attempted to turn the line printer into a Braille-producing machine. The period (".") was used to make the Braille cells. For example, IBM provided a special printer change and KIT adapter for the 1400 series of line printers and made Braille production possible.

Cultural barriers aside, a blind person with this technology now appeared capable of using a computer in every way that a sighted person could. However, as we moved into the realm of the cathode ray tube (CRT) computer terminal in the 1970's, a clamor went up from the blind community about the need to "make the CRT accessible." The principle issue with the accessibility of the CRT was the need to see the characters that are on the screen. Although this technological change necessitated some extra work for blind people, various devices quickly overcame the gap.

One of these devices was known as an OPTACON, for Optical to Tactile Converter. The OPTACON utilized a photoelectric camera with 144 photocells and a zoom lens. The signal from each cell was connected to a piezoelectric crystal that drove an individual vibrating rod up through a hole in a finger tray. The tray contained 144 holes with rods beneath them. The person using the OPTACON would place a finger on the tray and would use a camera in the other hand to scan across either a printed page or a CRT screen. The OPTACON would deliver to the finger tray the shapes of the letters being scanned. Since the letters were in the shape of printed characters, the OPTACON user had to be trained to recognize the printed shapes.

The OPTACON held quite a place in the blind community during the 1970's because, for the first time, blind people had a device that enabled them to read printed material. The main drawback of the OPTACON was that it could scan only one letter or character at a time. This meant that reading was slow and very labor-intensive. The top OPTACON reading speed records were about 60 words per minute. One idea that my colleagues and I explored at Lawrence Berkeley Laboratory and the University of Minnesota was to develop a special computer terminal that employed the OPTACON finger tray but did not require the user to scan a camera across a CRT screen. The user would rotate a flywheel attached to a digital shaft encoder; in turn, the encoder would address a character in memory and present its shape on the finger tray. This approach eliminated the need to lift a probe and scan it across a CRT screen. It also eliminated any tracking issues, since the user was always on a line of text.

With the advent of text-to-speech systems in the early 1980's, the computer terminal for the blind seemed to put the blind on equal footing with the sighted. Terminals were developed to enable blind people to read information in excess of 400 words per minute. Although the speech engines were monotone and sometimes the pronunciation was unclear, users didn't take long to get used to these systems.

When the PC came upon the scene, screen-reader programs were quickly developed, utilizing text-to-speech technology to permit the blind person to read any character information that was presented on the screen. Things went on swimmingly as long as people stayed in DOS on an IBM PC. Sure, there were graphics that could not be described by a screen reader but the basic operation of the computer and most applications—such as word processors, programming tools, and operating system functions—did not employ graphics.

Most blind people ignored the Macintosh when it was released in 1984 because it was not character-based. Soon after, though, a small group of blind people and programmers at Berkeley Systems developed a screen reader for the Mac,

Outspoken, that permits a blind person to utilize a number of applications. Icons can be recognized by the screen-reader software and assigned to words, such as "trash" for the trash can.

With the advent of Windows and graphics-oriented applications, the era of the text-based terminal has passed. Now we are in the age of the picture, and the picture is the primary view that is presented. In response, Sun Microsystems and Microsoft have developed accessibility interfaces that permit programmers to build an accessibility layer into applications. This layer is quite complicated, but put simply, the application sends a message to the screen reader whenever it opens a dialogue or a window.

The benefit of this accessibility layer is that it allows screen readers to describe the application's functionality. The problem is that the graphical and pictorial views of the application are ignored. If blind people are to use computers in the same manner as sighted people and to communicate fully, this problem must be solved.

I won't detail the various accessibility standards here, but I do want to provoke your thought with these questions:

- Is it important for blind people and sighted people to see the same picture?
- What is the picture really portraying?
- How can we design systems that are truly accessible and that communicate the same information to all?

These are not idle questions. The computer has evolved from being the financial calculator in the back office of a business to the information tether that connects society. We read our books, do our shopping, write our poems, and take our courses all with the aid of the computer.

It's my view that the Internet represents a greater revolution of information flow than did the Gutenberg printing press. Before the printing press, a few monks controlled information. With the advent of the Internet Web page, anyone can publish information that is immediately available to the entire world. A

15

key element to the success of any individual in our society, whether it pertains to the job, home life, family, parenting, or education, is the acquisition of information—not only in text form, but in the forms of pictures and sound, as well. Now, with virtual reality, we will be able to touch and smell over the Internet.

Think of the power that America Online has, and you'll get some understanding of the fight that some blind people are involved in. In the late 1990's, the National Federation of the Blind (NFB) brought suit against America Online because the software that it provides is not accessible to *any* screen reader. When someone develops a Web page, he or she has the choice to use images along with text. Depending on how the Web page is developed, it may or may not be accessible to blind people. One's choice to omit scannable text may be discriminatory, and that's what the NFB is trying to demonstrate in its lawsuit.

We are at an exciting crossroads in that the very need to solve the accessibility problem causes blind and sighted people to work together. We are only now getting at the true purpose of images and pictures. Although sighted people use pictures all the time, they do it so automatically that not much thought goes into the pictures' role in communication. When I was involved in developing various terminals for use by people who are blind, I had to learn how sighted people see objects and letters on the screen. The converse was true for the sighted people. They gained knowledge about how blind people interpret visual information. This learning process was key to our mutual understanding.

Looking back at how much the blind have accomplished in their work with computers—especially in their collaborations with the sighted—we can have high expectations of more solutions for accessibility in the coming years.

Solving Other People's Problems

Don Gray

A problem can be many things: a struggle, a puzzle, or a task. As a consultant, I find it useful to define the word as the difference between what is and what is wanted. From that point of view, learning to solve other people's problems means learning to connect with your clients and to understand what they think they have, what they think they want, and what they would like to do about it. The experience of living teaches each of us a lot about this kind of problem-solving, but the lessons are often murky. In recent years, I've been trying to become more conscious of my own process so that I can control and accelerate it. Here are some basic principles that I've found helpful.

The Pause Principle

When you encounter a problem, pause before trying to solve it.

The problem-solving starting point should be, "Don't just do something, stand there!" This principle is especially important when strong emotions are involved. It's downright critical when these strong emotions belong to you. Pausing creates space for a lot of things: to breathe, to center yourself, to let more information come to you, to notice that the problem is different than you first thought, or to notice a solution sitting in plain view. To pause is not to stop everything. You can be doing a lot of things while you're pausing. One of the most important is to pay attention.

The Pay Attention Principle

Critical information about the problem will hide in plain view.

I often find that what I need to know to solve a problem is not explicitly stated. But I also find that it's not always easy for me to hear information that I am told. Communication is a complicated process. One tool I use for checking the process is the Satir Interaction Model. This model decomposes communication into four parts: Intake, Meaning, Significance, and Response. Intake is what we physically see or hear. Meaning is the sum of ideas we think are conveyed by the message. Significance is how our interpretation of the message impacts us, our emotional reaction to it. Response is what we do in reply or as a reaction to the message. What I like about this model is that it helps me appreciate the many ways that good communication can go bad. If any part of this process goes wrong, the whole communication will be distorted in some way. Certain personality types may be more prone to mistakes in certain steps than are others. I occasionally jump too quickly into Response, before I've sorted out the other three parts of the process. Knowing that, I find that the Pause Principle helps me to give the process time and ultimately to pay better attention.

Communication is also important because of the next principle: Partnership.

The Partnership Principle

When I make the problem mine alone, I create more problems for all of us.

The problem I'm presented isn't really my problem. I am not in the middle of it, the other person is. So, there are risks whenever I try to help. By helping, I may

- deprive that person of a learning opportunity
- take time away from my work to do another's work
- encourage an ongoing co-dependency between my client and me
- find a "solution" that my client feels no connection with

The Partnership Principle reminds me to keep my client involved with the solving process. Ideally, my client will solve the problem and my role will be to support the effort. The worst case is when I find myself so involved in solving the problem myself that, by the time I unveil my wonderful solution, the client has forgotten about the problem and moved on. This situation relates to the next principle: Passion.

The Passion Principle

Don't care more about solving the problem than the other person does.

I once worked with a training company that I believed had a problem. Their training material was substandard, their trainer had never used the software, and they were losing money because the sales channel wouldn't promote the class. The client and I initially set out to solve this problem together. But less than a week after we dove in, I woke up and realized that I was the only one who cared about solving this problem. The client would not commit the resources to support a solution.

My visions of better training and a better training business notwithstanding, I had to scale down my own enthusiasm to match the client's lack of concern. A client who has no passion about a problem doesn't really have one. And when something's not a problem, it's not a problem not to solve it.

Passion does not belong to the intellect, so you can't solve important problems with intellect alone. You also have to connect emotionally, in some way. You have to see the people involved and find a way to appreciate how they see the world. This leads us to the next principle's focus: People.

The Person Principle

Every problem is a problem for some person.

Each of the principles above is a reflection of this one. To solve a problem well, you need to identify its owner and create a solution that works for that person. This is not so difficult if you are both the owner and the solver, but it gets tricky when you're trying to solve someone else's problems. Often, there are many more people involved than just the particular person who asked your help to solve it. Furthermore, you aren't only dealing with the people themselves and the problem itself, but also with how the people feel about the problem, about each other, about you, and about the attributes of whatever solution you recommend.

And that is your problem.

The Perils of Parallel Projects

Johanna Rothman

A recent client, Bob, asked me to assess a major project. "Johanna, it's so late, I don't know what to do. If we don't get it out on time, we'll miss the market window. I can't believe any of the estimates I get anymore. The project manager hasn't met a single deadline." I agreed to talk to the project manager, Sam, to find out what was happening.

I had some trouble making an appointment with him, but after a week, we arranged an in-person one-hour interview. Once we had settled down in a conference room, I started asking him questions about his project.

After I'd been there five minutes, a project member came in with a burning question. Sam excused himself and talked to the employee for a few minutes.

We started to talk again, but someone from another project came in with an urgent question. Sam excused himself again and solved the crisis.

Two more crises interrupted us.

Within an hour, four people had crises that only Sam could solve. Four different projects—and only Sam could help!

I stopped the project-specific interview and asked Sam these questions:

- How many projects are you managing?
- Are you happy with that?

Sam frowned and said, "I'm managing only four projects. But that seems to be three more than I can handle." I asked if we could talk uninterrupted for twenty minutes, and he said we could. We took a walk, to get uninterrupted time.

After I talked to Sam, I went back to Bob and said, "I know how to solve your project problem." He was amazed. "Johanna, you've only spent about an hour here. How could you possibly figure out what was going on in that time?" I explained that I could not understand the projects in that time, but I could understand what was happening to the project staff.

Sam had been the original architect on Project A. He was now managing a later release of Project A and managing early releases of Projects B, C, and D. The company had shipped Project A before it was completely frozen, so after the initial release, they had more defects to find and fix in Project A. Projects B, C, and D used components from the same code base as Project A. Whenever Project A ran into trouble, the staff called on Sam to help. Delays on Project A delayed Projects B, C, and D.

Sam was also making project-wide decisions about Projects B, C, and D. He was on the critical path for all four projects. Sam realized this and tried to give each project about 25 percent of his time. During our walk, he told me he didn't have much to do on each of the projects; he just had to clean up a few things and then manage the projects. After all, he said, if he spent just over a day per week on each of them, he would be out of this mess in a week or two. I asked him how long this shell game had gone on. He looked at me sheepishly and said, "About six weeks."

Six weeks ago, Sam hadn't been able to free up more than two hours at a time on each of the projects, but he thought he could fix that in the next week. Five weeks ago, Sam hadn't been able to free up more than one-and-a-half hours at a time for any of the projects. Each week, he spent less and less uninterrupted time on each of the projects.

All of Sam's deliverables were late and all the projects were late because Sam had not been able to dedicate enough time to any of them when it was needed. Sam was unable to spend an entire day on any given project. He was constantly interrupted. He repeatedly switched context: He stopped what he was doing, remembered what someone had requested, did it, and then went back to what he was doing. Instead of 25 percent of Sam on all four projects, the company was getting about 5 to 10 percent of Sam on all projects. (See Table 1, contrasting the number of assigned tasks with the percentage of available time a person could spend on each task.)

Table 1: *Number of tasks and actual time available to spend on each task. Source: Gerald M. Weinberg,* Quality Software Management, Vol. 1: Systems Thinking *(New York: Dorset House Publishing, 1992), p. 284.*

Number of Tasks	Percent of Time on Each
1	100
2	40
3	20
4	10
5	5
more than 5	random

I went back to Bob and explained that context-switching led to a reduction in people's performance. He said, "Well, if I take Sam off two projects and leave him on two, will that help?" I said it would help but he still wouldn't be getting half of Sam on each project; he would be getting closer to 40 percent of Sam per project. I told Bob he should decide which project had the highest priority and have Sam work full-time on that project, then on the next-highest-priority project, and so on, until Sam could finish his critical-path work.

Bob reluctantly agreed to do this. Without interruptions, Sam was able to complete his critical-path work for all four projects in the next seven working days. He was then able to focus his energies on the project management tasks.

Sam's context-switching had been caused by chronically understaffed projects. Bob understaffed his projects by design. He had his reasons: the difficulty of hiring people; his preference for a sense of urgency around projects; and the feeling that if everyone was completely busy all the time, he was getting maximum value for his personnel dollars.

By creating a shortfall of people to staff projects, Bob insured that each project would start with insufficient staff. Every project was staffed with portions of people's time. Since each person had multiple responsibilities, each person decided when to work on which project. As a result, Bob's organization could not take a consistent approach to projects and every project was late.

Bob was concerned that if he made choices about which project was more important, the less-important projects would not be done. I explained that he was ranking projects *at a given time*, and that his rankings would change over time. He had to make that clear to his staff, but I was sure the staff would understand. Ranking each project, even temporarily, helped the entire organization work together.

People do not switch contexts easily. It is more productive for people to continue working on the same project, at the same level, for as long as possible. Switching to another project or activity costs time and brainpower. Rank your projects, and make sure people know what they need to do and when. Make sure people work in whole-person increments, if you want to get the most out of your people.

Do I Want to Take This Crunch Project?

Sharon Marsh Roberts and Ken Roberts

You've been thrown into a project that will have highly visible results of success or failure and a deadline that looks much too aggressive. How do you respond?

This essay explores the danger signs and the success factors that will help you decide whether to accept a project, reduce its scope, adjust its resources, or step aside. We use the following five questions to address these issues:

- How do I know it's a crunch project?
- How do I consider the choice?
- What's the impact on the other key players?
- Can I shape the project into something that works for me?
- What else should I know?

First, you need to discern whether or not the project is what we call a "crunch" project.

How Do I Know It's a Crunch Project?

A crunch project is best identified by two requirements or constraints:

1. There are major negative consequences if the project's deadline is not met.
2. Given the constraints of the project, the allocated resources (time, money, or people) are significantly smaller than those required to fulfill the needs of the sponsor and the customers.

Now, you might say, "That sounds like the definition of a *hopeless* project." Well, there surely are hopeless projects, and if you can discern that the project you face is hopeless, we suggest you distance yourself from it quickly.

But by "crunch project," we imagine something different: a risky project that might succeed under better conditions than those currently presented by management. In such a project, some of the constraints can be changed and some significant risk can be accepted, making the project more of a sensible bet. Management might commit to support such changes because the consequences of project failure are significant.

So, as we discuss later, ascertain whether or not the terms are negotiable. If management won't budge, the project will fail. Explore with management the opportunities for change. Until you (and your managers) answer the questions posed in this essay, we wouldn't bet on the success of your project.

It May Be a Pseudo-Crunch

Sometimes, projects masquerade as crunch projects. In many organizations these days, management sets up every systems effort as if it were a crunch project or a *death march*.

Usually, the masquerade takes the form of a *pseudo-deadline*. Internal management picks a date, but there are no significant impacts on profits or external relationships if the date is missed.

And usually behind the pseudo-deadline is a *pseudo-customer*. A real customer can choose not to undertake a project. A pseudo-customer cannot. Often, the pseudo-customer of a systems project is a group in the same business unit as the systems organization. The systems organization is the vendor of choice within the business unit. Often, a pseudo-customer will insulate the business from the system so that the business will only suffer hurt feelings if the effort fails. Such hurt feelings can be managed politically, unlike bottom-line consequences of a failed crunch project.

A less typical case we encountered involved the CEO of an entire enterprise. In a meeting with the project sponsor and the leader of the intended project, he announced his desire for a new method of evaluating business unit performance. The CEO emphasized his great desire that this project be implemented in time for the next project planning cycle. In the months that followed, the project leader began to assertively implement the required measures to meet the CEO's goal. But the project sponsor hesitated to support any change that offended or interfered with a subsidiary's operations. Progress waned. Finally, as the CEO became embroiled with more urgent issues, progress on this project nearly halted. Ultimately, it slipped past the next planning cycle.

Why the Difference Matters

If your project is truly a crunch project, your team can expect not only extraordinary required effort, but also commensurate recognition of its accomplishments. In a pseudo-crunch, the team will be disappointed. Hardly anyone in the company will acknowledge the team's effort or results. The stress of these conditions may impact your health and your family—and your team's health. The project may seem endless.

Sometimes, in order to push the project forward fast enough, you will have to make enemies outside the team or even within it. If the project is ultimately a pseudo-crunch, you'll realize that there was no justification for destroying your relationships.

In other words, a pseudo-crunch brings real personal losses, with no balancing gains.

Spotting a True Crunch

In addition to the two requirements and constraints mentioned earlier, a real crunch has two readily observable characteristics:

- There is a *measurable impact* on money (profit, revenue, or expenses) or an impact that has observable results on a relationship with an important outside party.
- There is *documented recognition* across the organizations involved that the results of this project have measurable impact.

By "measurable impact," we mean that somebody actually creates a model that expresses how dollars relate to success versus delay or failure. Ideally, such a model would express a cost per day for a delay in the project. The cost of delays relates to some external party, often the customer of the goods or services of the company. This measurement is especially important in the competitive climate created by the Internet. Another important source of hard deadlines can be a government regulatory agency. Our ability to measure effects in dollars does not require absolute precision, but it does require a keen sense of direction and orders of magnitude of the consequences.

By "documented recognition," we mean that you and your boss aren't the only ones who think the project has a major impact. Press releases are good evidence of recognition, as are government edicts, but contractual commitments with an outside party are also sufficient evidence of recognition.

Examples of true crunch projects include the following:

A new line of business: A mortgage lender began accepting home mortgage applications over the phone. This focus changed the company's primary customer from a corporation paying for relocation to a consumer intending to close on a house. Such customers required quick turnaround, with each week of delay reducing the probability of a closing. The head of marketing had proposed a system to automate the end-to-end application process. He estimated that the volume of closed mortgages per week would increase by four million dollars if the time to close a mortgage were dropped from three weeks to one-and-a-half weeks. When the new automated system was installed, the company captured 50 percent of the existing market from a world-famous lender and exceeded its revenue estimates for the first year. This growth was achieved by approving mortgages roughly five to seven days faster than the competitor.

Regulatory response: The U.S. Food and Drug Administration instituted a financial disclosure requirement for pharmaceutical researchers when they file for the approval of a new drug. Since a delay in application would cost a major drug maker approximately one million dollars per day, pharmaceutical companies immediately began analyzing financial disclosure processes.* A major pharmaceutical company defined the disclosure system as a key system, but encountered problems in creating a costly Web-based, multi-user application. The analysis team solved the crunch by building an interim system in Microsoft Access, Excel, and Word. The interim system brought the company successfully through at least six filings in the six months that followed, without a single day of delay.

---

* The real cost is higher at the early end, when the lack of competitors can create a lock on the market. Once a physician becomes accustomed to writing "sertraline" or "Zoloft" every time he or she sees a depressed patient, it's hard to get that physician to prescribe a new drug.

29

How Do I Consider the Choice?

Once you've determined whether or not the project is a crunch, you must weigh the consequences of accepting it.

First, Determine That You Have a Choice

Knowing that you have a choice is important. You can negotiate effectively if you believe you have a choice. Without it, you will concede on vital issues in the first negotiations, perhaps with irreparable consequences. Often, the initial conditions are critical to the success of the project. Further down the timeline of the project, additional critical issues may arise.

If you sense a lack of choice, consider it your first major warning sign that the project is not a crunch—it's hopeless. Your feeling is a good reason to look for a way to walk away from the project.

Those without choices have no power. Those without power cannot change ill-fated projects.

Keep Your Options Open

It's difficult to maintain your power to choose while other players are asserting their definition of the project and its boundaries. Nobody is looking out for your choices, so it's easy to feel as if you don't have many—or any—choices that matter.

Here are some ideas for how to find and nurture your power to choose:

1. Get away to a different place—different from work, especially, but also away from other places with people who impose the constraints you feel. Paradoxically, despite the time-pressure crunch projects impose, they may require you to take time away to meditate, to exercise, and to clear your mind.

2. Write down what choices you feel you do have, and what choices you feel you do not have. Three key options to consider are finding another job, refusing the project, or suggesting someone else to take some major pieces of the project.
3. Write down how you see the opportunities and risks of the main choices, and how the risks feel to you. Is this project somebody else's big chance? Will the rewards of this project motivate you to continue when things get painful and crazy later—when your team is counting on you to sustain *them?*
4. Get another person outside the project to look at what you've written. Talk with a trusted outsider and allow him or her to help you think about the possibilities. Often when you're under pressure, your vision of alternatives may be blocked.

Once you've found a new choice, talk to people who can support you in this path. Allow them to provide practical assistance as well as emotional support. Being the lonely hero looks good in movies, but most of us cannot resolutely stand alone. Don't hesitate to return to your support person or persons during the project. You may need to review your options periodically—for the sake of sanity and health. If you lack support in your efforts, you may not be able to participate in such an intense project in the first place.

Sometimes managers convince malleable employees (and consultants) to make promises and commitments early in the project. Sometimes we give away choices by committing to others' desires. It's important not to give away choices, and to agree only to commitments with ample rewards. Don't make unconditional commitments. It's good to be supportive of your management as long as they are supportive of you, but not longer. Retain your power to choose. You don't know what conditions will befall the project later. Many a project team has survived its management, through mergers, acquisitions, reorganizations, and other events. These events can make even the most necessary of projects irrelevant or impossible. And any such event may invalidate management's promises. Often, new management will reevaluate projects for expense and risk. Troubled systems projects become easy targets for termination, as do their creators and builders.

What's the Impact on the Other Key Players?

Even if a project feels like it could work for you personally, it's not going to succeed unless the other key players are also personally committed. Look specifically at these key players: the outside parties, the sponsor, the other internal stakeholders, and your team.

Outside Parties

Outside parties are typically customers or government regulators. Other parties are powerful suppliers or employee groups. Consider carefully these risks:

1. Customers who lack a contract or a track record on previous projects may not remain committed to intended outcomes in the face of change.
2. Major customers or groups of customers with fundamentally different interests may eventually agree to disagree about product requirements. Their resources may be transferred to different projects. Or the customers may never reach a consensus or develop a stable set of requirements to finish the project.
3. Many a government regulator has changed course after significant lobbying or other political events. On these issues, it's important to read newspapers and to stay abreast of current events. In the case of the new pharmaceutical regulation, the press was filled with stories about clerical investigators who manipulated research data and dramatically raised the prices they charged the pharmaceutical companies for each patient studied.

The Sponsor

The sponsor has the budget and the authority to take action. He or she represents the project to top management (sometimes as a member of top management) and to outside parties and, as sponsor, will be held accountable for the project results. Sponsors don't focus on one project full-time, because they have responsibility for other projects and organizations, too.

You should get some key information from or about the key sponsor. Start with this question:

> Has the sponsor ever accomplished a project with crucial attributes similar to yours—attributes that include the following?

- a project or activity that is really new for their organization, rather than an incremental improvement
- a project or activity that creates a new entity or environment
- a project or activity that would have failed without the real buy-in of several other organizations
- a major systems change that actually impacts business processes or the activities of outside entities, rather than a change affecting internal systems, sometimes invisible to the user

Your risk is that you're working with someone who hasn't considered the project and its consequences. Even worse, the sponsor may choose to remain isolated, avoiding any coaching you offer. While this project may become the source of great personal growth for this sponsor, the burden of supporting the sponsor's education may fall entirely on you.

Follow up with more questions:

> Is the sponsor willing to make decisions that don't please everyone?

Does the sponsor see the need to protect the team and the customers?

Crunch projects often require clear but imperfect decisions, made immediately and with no regrets.

The sponsor you don't want is a high-level manager with a reputation for *niceness*, having avoided being the bad guy throughout his or her career. Such managers provide support in good times, but nice guys avoid conflict and leave the risks to others. Some people are truly risk-averse and are thus ill-suited for risky projects.

Your goal is to protect yourself (and your team, if possible). If your sponsor cannot do the hard work of managing organizational consequences and expectations, you cannot succeed in executing the essential details of the plan.

Other Internal Stakeholders

Other internal stakeholders include the sponsor's potential adversaries or allies.

The sponsor has what it takes to make the project go. The other stakeholders can make the project stop—either by withholding a critical sign-off or by withholding a key specialized resource. Some are business people; others are technical (like the person who knows the interface of a system from which your new system must get data).

Some key questions about other internal stakeholders are: Who is peripherally involved or affected? What opportunities and risks are associated with the project from each party's perspective? (The project's risk may in fact be an outsider's opportunity—someone may gain headcount and domain if the project fails.) What are the personal and business histories between the internal stakeholders and the sponsor? (More than one project's demise has resulted from a past feud between two powerful managers.) Does your sponsor have the ability to keep feuding stakeholders from blocking the project?

Your Team

The team members may have different backgrounds, as long as they can work together. In order to build the energy needed to succeed on a real crunch project, the team must have

- full-time focus on the project
- very strong communication, working face-to-face in one location
- freedom from distractions, including from each other, the infrastructure, or the political history
- all the key skills and knowledge and stakeholder connections required to complete the project

One More Question

Were there any previous attempts to do this project? Project failures are fairly commonplace, as are second and third attempts. Often, management is enthusiastic about implementing lessons learned from previous attempts and is ready to embark on the next version of a risky project.

A project with a history of failure has a large, extra psychological burden: fear. Unfortunately, fear is a potent motivator of risk avoidance, but not of creative analysis. Teams may be justified in being afraid of a project. Management often learns the wrong lessons and discovers new or different ways to fail. What management learns is dependent on its readiness to learn. If management has not learned some fundamentals of project management, the more complex lessons will be misunderstood or missed entirely.

If you are starting a second (or third or even subsequent) iteration of a project, take the time to review the previous results with as many participants and observers as you can. Look for any showstoppers that really haven't changed. Evaluate management's readiness for the project at the same time that management evaluates your capabilities.

35

Can I Shape the Project Into Something That Works for Me?

A crunch project requires shaping—such as adjustments to the project scheduling, staffing, or resources. The project's current terms and conditions are a probable route to failure. Your strategy should be to use the probability of failure to awaken management. Management needs to avoid the consequences of such failure. You need to change management's assumption that the project will turn out well in the end.

What You Can Accomplish: Your Own Power

The key to all this renegotiation is your knowledge of yourself. Who are you? What do you want? If you know what you want, you can negotiate effectively. Renegotiating a faulty project plan is a necessity. To renegotiate the project, you need to be certain of what ends are necessary. If some end is critical but management is uninspired to change, can you walk away? Can you work around the worst of the damage? Can you inspire others to support you? Can you jointly find a way to solve the problem? The wrong answer (following the present course) may be more obvious than any right answer, so creativity is required.

Effective Re-Shaping and Negotiation

Because high-risk projects rarely catch up, you should act as soon as possible. The biggest difference between a high-risk project and a normal project is that there is a smaller margin for error in the former. The lessons learned within the project become critical as the time to absorb them shortens. So, the focus needs to be on doing things right—now, not later.

You need the power to demand management's permission to take action:

- You need to talk directly with the outside customers or stakeholders.

- You need to reduce the scope to the essentials that deliver urgent value, as perceived by the sponsor and the outside stakeholders or customers. You'll need the sponsor and customers to quantify (or at least to state precisely) what terrible consequences will ensue if a particular deliverable is not available by its due date.
- You need to have the right team, started up the right way. Most importantly, you need the right to *refuse* a problem person that some organization is dumping on you.
- You and your team need to be provided with the right motivational structure, such as in terms of performance measurements.

Any project requires direct communication, a competent team, and a reasonable scope. Lever the crunch to get what your project requires.

Get Management Support

Management may, under extraordinary circumstances, accede to all you ask. Or management may agree to some critical changes. If management agrees to change the conditions that present the most difficulty in the project, then you've established the right kind of communication.

Management may instead respond with an offer of certain "concessions"—conditions other than those you requested, changes that are less important to the project. If you don't go into your discussion with management knowing which changes are critical, you may fall prey to this tendency of management.

When management responds to your requests, you need to evaluate these responses. Has management provided enough support for you to start the project? Do you need to present new arguments for greater changes to the project? How soon must you get your managers' agreement on any one concern?

Your goal is difficult—to keep management's attention and commitment to the project throughout its duration.

Management may say, "No, we can't afford what you ask." This response may reveal that it is a lower priority. Perhaps the project is not a crunch project after all. Maybe your managers want to squeeze more productivity from you and your team. Management may be taking its chances on the consequences, or may simply have no clue how hard this project is.

If the answer on changes is no, allow management to run the project according to its own judgment and to learn some hard lessons—with someone else as project leader. Sometimes, you can position yourself as the more prudent project leader, to be considered as a replacement when this effort fails and management wishes to try a second time. But for now, the implication of no is that you can't afford this project. You need to go back and take a good look at your alternative actions.

Modify the Scope of the Project

Often, management says that the scope of the deliverables cannot be reduced. The project goes forward under wishful thinking. In many cases, the most important step toward making a project succeed is for the sponsor (and the customers and other stakeholders) to recognize that the original scope is hopeless. If the sponsor will consider your suggestions for alternative goals, you can creatively negotiate a less elegant solution with a higher probability of success.

For example, on an executive compensation project for a large financial services company, many deliverables were listed in the original requirements and the initial project effort stalled. We came in as the second team and asked, "Which capabilities are absolutely necessary for you to get through year-end with this system?" The absolute requirement was a stream of transactions to be added to the executive payroll, along with reports that detailed the rewards for the employee and the human resources (HR) management. This stream of transactions would initiate all short- and long-term awards.

With that realization, any other transaction or report became a "nice to have." The lead business analyst from our team executed the remaining transactions manually during year-end and compiled the data that would be needed for other reports. The programming team still worked eighty-hour weeks to complete work on the modified scope, but year-end was a success. The numerous additional processes and reports were programmed throughout the next year and were available to the system for the following year-end compensation cycle.

Create a Subproject to Manage a Reduced Scope

The modification to scope in the example above was implemented with full knowledge and agreement of management. That agreement was made because management understood the gap between what was wanted and what was possible. Sometimes management is not ready to admit its overexuberance, but is willing to afford alternatives.

In the case of the pharmaceutical company's new obligation to report financial interests of investigators to the FDA, management believed the fully automated system could be implemented. However, to hedge their bets, the managers agreed to create a separate interim project within a user team composed of analysts and users. The user team agreed that a contingency plan was needed, so it proceeded in parallel with the systems project team. Once the users became more conversant with their desktop tools, including database design tools, they designed and created a semi-automated system using Microsoft Access, Excel, and Word. Data were downloaded from the critical regulatory and financial systems and were input from paper forms. The automated system was expected in June of 1999 (and had not been produced as of early 2000). The interim system has functioned throughout 1999 and in 2000, allowing filings to be completed and to reach the FDA on schedule. The interim project provided a better understanding of the problem and also protected the company from the financial impact of a delayed filing.

Sometimes management is not ready to give overt permission to reduce scope, but will accept alternatives as delivered. If you cannot get management's explicit agreement to reduce scope, consider the following strategy: Deliver what you and the critical users agree is essential first, knowing that later delivery of the less essential deliverables may be cancelled. If you take this strategy, you should be prepared to follow through and complete the less essential deliverables, not because they are important to the system or the users, but because management deems the less essential elements as part of their agreement with you.

Modify the Team

Even if the team comes pre-assembled and you keep every member, you have to go through a sign-on process with each person. Never assume that because staff members were handed to you they will automatically accept your leadership. Perhaps your most important powers are to accept each person who is committed to the project and to veto any person who is likely to block the whole energy of your team.

Take a Different Role

Don't define yourself by what management expects. Define yourself by what you know to be your best fit.

Ideally, find the role or roles that suit you, and delegate or assign the rest of the responsibilities to other people. The sponsor of the executive compensation project mentioned earlier was a well-known HR manager with little systems background. She faced an internally produced design and limited internal resources to develop the system. She accepted the assignment—but made a request for outside resources and enlisted internal systems resources to qualify the outside bidders. She assembled the most critical internal resources, with both business and technical expertise, to provide support during development. Thus, she used her understanding of staffing processes to assume a role that was new for her, managing a systems-development effort.

You might not be the right person to lead this crunch project. You might be uncomfortable with the risk. Perhaps you are not able to get free from other responsibilities to focus all your time and energy on the project. Or perhaps you have some negative history with a key player who will not give credibility to your suggestions. Maybe you are insufficiently motivated by the rewards offered by management to sign on.

Sometimes you can refer the project to another internal person without hurting your career. You might retain a role as some kind of representative for your organization or advisor on certain topics.

If you have budgetary control or influence, another approach is for you to consider engaging a project manager who is not an employee of the organization. Outsiders are often more able to work with the required risk, time focus, and reward structure, and at the same time they are free from political conflicts in your organization. Your role can then be that of an overseer, liaison, and quality-control expert.

What Else Should I Know?

Each crunch project is different from every other one, but most are complicated, somewhat intimidating, and exciting. These complications may create further questions and interesting discussions of your project. In fact, we'd like to hear about them. So, by all means, send your thoughts, concerns, or puzzles to us at Sharon@Roberts-1.com.

To read a fascinating book about crunch projects, try *Death March*, by Ed Yourdon. For help in really getting to the heart of a problem project, read *Are Your Lights On?*, by Donald C. Gause and Gerald M. Weinberg, or other books by Gerald M. Weinberg.

If you'd like to get involved in discussions about a wider range of topics on projects and systems in human organizations, we recommend that you check out the SHAPE forum (for

Software as a Human Activity Performed Effectively) on www.geraldmweinberg.com.

We haven't covered every question about crunch projects in this essay, and certainly we have not provided every answer. Your mission is to explore the assumptions about your crunch project, to seek out new choices and opportunities, and to boldly negotiate those choices with management.

Part Two:
Improving
Interpersonal
Interactions

A recurring dream of technical workers is to have the opportunity to work in perfect isolation. For better or worse, though, the vast majority of technical work puts us in relationships with other people. So, if we are to amplify our effectiveness, we must learn how to amplify the effectiveness of our interpersonal interactions.

The job of software architect is a perfect example. Though many of us perceive the architect as a solitary individual laboring in an ivory tower, Bob King disabuses us of that primitive notion with his essay on measuring the effectiveness of his architectural work. All of his measures, in the end, are measures of his effectiveness at working with others.

In her two contributions, Naomi Karten shows us how to build strong working relationships and how to transform relationships that are threatened by anger, especially those with irate customers. Becky Winant warns us of some tempting maneuvers that can destroy a team's working relationships, and Jerry Weinberg recommends interviewing by audition as a way to start good relationships with new employees or team members.

Life as a Software Architect

Bob King

The first time I noticed the pattern of the following conversation, I had just joined a project that was foundering. I was unpacking my things and placing them in my new cubicle when one of the developers approached me. We introduced ourselves, and he welcomed me warmly to the project. Then he asked, "What's your role on the project?"

"I'm the architect," I said.

He looked at me blankly.

"I'm responsible for figuring out what the pieces are, how they fit together, and how to approach the whole thing. And I am responsible for communicating this, and issues that come up surrounding it, to the project manager and other management types. I'm kind of a high-level designer."

"Oh," he said, "I understand. I just wanted to make sure we won't be doing redundant work."

He said he understood, but he didn't look or sound like he did. He slipped away awkwardly, and I knew that I hadn't really made contact.

45

What Architects Try to Do

That was only one of many times I've had trouble giving a crisp description of what I do as a software architect. My explanation sounded soft and ethereal—and incomplete. Maybe it was soft and ethereal because software architecture starts at a very high level. Maybe it was incomplete because I had trouble succinctly describing architecture's interpersonal aspects. Maybe it wasn't understood because I didn't really understand it.

Whether I understand it or not, I *know* that good architecture is critical to the success of any complex software project. That's why I've struggled over the years to clarify my thinking. What *is* software architecture, and if I do it, how do I know I'm doing it well?

When I'm the architect on a software project, I work to envision, communicate, and refine the form of the software solution. Initially, the form of the software solution may be nothing more than a set of design principles or a picture with some number of items and relationships among them. Here are some examples of design principles:

- The technical review committee must review all design work.
- The existing application logic and databases (data structures and data) will be migrated into the new environment.
- The new application will move toward being fully Web-enabled.
- A multitiered architecture will be implemented to separate data presentation, business logic, and data access and update.
- Oracle products will be used as much as possible.

As I iterate through the process, I add sufficient detail to these principles and pictures so my work can become the basis for the detailed design of the software.

Whom do I work with? As much as I would sometimes like it, this work is not done in a vacuum. I work to satisfy the requirements and constraints provided by business stakeholders and sponsors, the project manager and IT management, and the development staff.

What are the constraints? The business stakeholders and sponsors want to know their problem will be solved. They want assurance that the solution won't cause other problems that might offset its value. The project manager and IT management want to predict how much the solution will cost to build and operate and what kinds of people and resources are required. They want to be warned if it won't fit within the current technical environment. The development staff is eager to know whether or not they can build it.

In order to reconcile these constraints, I must first understand requirements, issues, and political nuances from all three perspectives, then mold them into at least one workable solution. This is not merely an intellectual task. If I cannot work incrementally, honestly, and openly with these three groups, I will fail. If I cannot present my ideas clearly to the key people, I will fail. If I cannot listen carefully to their reactions, I will fail. And if I don't work hard to gain their trust and respect, I'll be out the door before I even have a chance to fail.

The Technical Trap

I now understand that being an architect is a leadership role, and that can be daunting for a technical type like me. When people issues become too much for me, I sometimes retreat into the safety of a good technical problem—a trap that lures many technical leaders. When working with a good technical problem, I get immediate feedback, and it's usually unambiguous. Not so, when working with human beings.

To help me avoid this technical trap, I created three key metrics:

- The Visibility Ratio

- The Conflict Metric
- The Anxiety Metric

Let's examine each one in turn.

The Visibility Ratio

This metric is the ratio of the time I actually spend with the key audiences versus the time I *need* to spend with them. For example, if I need to spend an hour per working day but get only a single one-hour meeting per week, my Visibility Ratio is one fifth—not very good at all.

Of course, I can't always know in advance how much time I'll need. Even when I do know how much, I can't always get it. I'm most successful at maintaining a high Visibility Ratio when I can leverage project structures that are already in place. For example, if the project has regular steering committee meetings, I campaign for a regular place on the agenda.

To support my Visibility Ratio, I ask for a formal partnership with the project manager—who may react to this request with suspicion. Some project managers are not accustomed to technical people asking for visibility with key management people, so I must pose this request delicately. If the project manager reacts with turf-guarding defenses, I consider this a strong sign that the project is not a fit for me. I've experienced projects in which the technical people were expected to act like nice children—seen but not heard—so I know I'll be ineffective without direct access to various business partners.

For example, while interviewing for one new project, I explained to the project manager, Rhoda, that the project architect should *not* report to her, but to her boss. Initially, Rhoda didn't take too kindly to my suggestion, but I suspected that my Visibility Ratio would be too low and that I couldn't do the architect's job while reporting through her. When I said that I wouldn't take the job under any other arrangement, Rhoda and her boss decided to take a chance. Rhoda and I, as the project manager and the project architect, were introduced to the project as peers.

To Rhoda's surprise, we worked well together. For example, we attended project steering committee meetings as a team. My role was to present high-level information about the approach we were taking. Rhoda presented information regarding project cost, schedule, and resources. Working as a team, we were able to address issues earlier in the process—and with more clarity. We eliminated the ineffective game of "telephone," in which project managers and their bosses present technical ideas rather than having those technical ideas presented directly by the technical staff. In the end, we worked as a team and succeeded as a team.

Sometimes, though, my Visibility Ratio suffers from having too much contact with the wrong people. For instance, when it's early in a project and I trap myself in endless technology-related discussions with developers, I know that my visibility to the other two audiences—managers and business stakeholders—must be suffering. I strive to get early feedback from developers about my current state of thinking, but awareness of my Visibility Ratio prevents me from getting snared in the technical trap.

The Conflict Metric

This metric measures the amount of strong feeling I uncover while I work. For instance, on the surface, the domain of the project architect is technical, but every technical design has business ramifications. When I have the visibility I need, I can work with the people who understand those business ramifications. I enter this arena fully aware that there will be places where conflict lurks below the surface. The sooner these conflicts surface, and are resolved, the better for the project, so if the Conflict Metric seems too low, I suspect that I don't yet understand all of the project's business ramifications.

I have not always believed that visible conflict is a good sign for an architect. Fearing conflict, I felt the emotional price

49

I paid for stirring up conflict exceeded any possible benefit. I felt safer avoiding conflict, but the safety was an illusion. Those happy projects were more fun—until all the bottled-up issues blew up in my face. Because I can still lapse into conflict avoidance, I regularly check the Conflict Metric to keep me on the rocky, but correct, path.

For instance, as I'm creating the form of a solution, I can immediately see some areas of the architecture that will ignite or create interpersonal tension. In other areas, however, I may be unsure about what emotional undercurrents may affect the project, so that's where I focus my early efforts. I form a tentative hypothesis—a description of some changes I may suggest —and I list the related advantages and disadvantages. Then I present the hypothesis to as many people as I can and carefully note their emotional reactions. I'm often surprised by what causes the conflicts, but reflecting on the source of the strong feelings always leads me to new and important information.

Exposing and dealing with conflict successfully is outside the scope of this essay. Two particularly good books are *Flawless Consulting,* by Peter Block, and *Becoming a Technical Leader,* by Gerald M. Weinberg (actually, almost any of Jerry's books are wonderful references for this topic).

The Anxiety Metric

Whereas the Conflict Metric measures external conflict, the Anxiety Metric measures internal stress. Whenever I perceive that some arbitrary commitments are imposed on the project and are creating a problem that exceeds the team's capability to deliver a solution, I become anxious. In any project, some trade-offs have to be made because not all of the initial requirements and constraints can be satisfied simultaneously. As an architect, my job is to identify such trade-offs, but sometimes I cannot get an acknowledgment from business or project management. Instead, they demand that the architect and developers somehow defy the laws of nature—and my Anxiety Metric shoots off the scale.

When I get into these situations, I find it easy to blame business or project management for my predicament. Once I start blaming people, it's easy to give up and work alone until the inevitable problems explode and can no longer be ignored. Then I emerge from my cocoon and participate in crisis-mode project management. Decisions are made to get something—anything—done, regardless of quality. When I do this, I have failed in my job as architect.

Although my anxiety initially stems from these arbitrary commitments, the ultimate source of my anxiety is my inability to communicate what is going on inside of me—anxiety about feeling anxious and not being able to tell anyone. My Anxiety Metric helps me escape this conundrum. When I become aware that my anxiety is high, I pause to identify the leading cause of my anxiety. Once I've identified the cause, I find the person who has the best chance of doing something to relieve it. Then I try to say, in my terms, what is bothering me—without blaming that person for how I feel. Doing this is very hard, but if I don't do it, my anxiety merely continues to grow.

For example, at the start of one project, the IT vice president, Frank, arbitrarily and unilaterally decided that a client management application should be purchased. The project was working to establish a virtual bank as a new division of a very large financial institution. I was on a team responsible for putting in place the technical architecture to support the bank's operation; I was on loan from an internal division that already had a strong client-management application—call it CMA.

We undertook an evaluation process that included CMA and a few other products. The process was a sham. Frank had already decided on his choice of vendor. The leading source of my anxiety was that this VP had railroaded me into not giving CMA a fair hearing. Realizing this, I worked with Frank to address my concerns. He exhibited a passive-aggressive stance with me. In our conversations, he placated me with prospects of a change in the evaluation process. However, no changes ever followed, and my anxiety increased.

My teammates and I largely gave up—having failed in our jobs as project architects. Failing is a part of life and, sometimes, life is too short to fight battles like these. However, I felt that I needed to take the next step, which was to bring the sham process to the attention of his and my management. I wrote my own evaluation of CMA, based on the requirements of the project at that time. I concluded that the project should implement CMA and mapped out the beginning of the process for doing that. I sent it to Frank, his boss, and his boss's boss, along with copies to my management.

That action was my last one on that project. Management removed me from my role as architect. The project—and the virtual bank itself—failed, and the VP was eventually fired. I am not sure—even to this day—if I sent my evaluation because I felt I could change the VP's mind. I know, however, that by being aware of my anxiety and by taking action, my anxiety did decrease.

The Definition of a Software Architect

My three metrics are not unrelated; they build upon one another. The Visibility Ratio helps to ensure that I have the kind of context that enables me to perform as project architect. The Conflict Metric helps to ensure that I am actually doing the important work rather than merely avoiding conflict. The Anxiety Metric helps to ensure that I am emotionally capable of finishing the work, not trapped by my fear of expressing myself.

When I pay attention to these measures, I prompt myself to do the right thing. If I'm not paying attention, the anxiety I feel usually awakens me. If I'm not stirring up conflict, I examine my current ideas, discover some areas that I haven't sufficiently explored, and work to probe those areas with new hypotheses. If I'm not getting the visibility I need, I try harder to get out and talk to the key people about what's bothering me.

With the help of my three measures, I have now developed an understanding that leads to a crisp definition of what I do as a project architect:

> I work with the key people on a project to agree upon a workable technical framework and an approach to implement a software solution. My effectiveness depends on how well I manage the access I have to stakeholders, the conflicts that arise during the design phase, and the anxiety I sense in response to unreasonable conditions.

Step One in Building Strong Working Relationships

Naomi Karten

At a national conference in Atlanta, I sat next to a woman I'd never seen before. We started chatting. She said she had spent most of her life in the Northeast.

"Same for me," I said. "Whereabouts?"

She said she was born in Connecticut.

"Gee, me too. Where?"

"New Haven," she said.

"Really? So was I."

"Yes," she told me. "I was born in New Haven Hospital."

"So was I!" I said, almost jumping out of my seat.

I'd love to report that we were born on the same day, but no, it wasn't even the same year. In fact, it'll be a decade until she's as old as I am, and by then, I'll be a decade older. Still, what are the odds that two total strangers have something so personal in common?

I believe the odds are high. While immersed in the squabbles and stresses of the typical workday, we sometimes become so focused on our differences that it's hard to believe we're alike in any way at all. But in fact, any two of us, or any three, or even any five or ten, have more in common than we might ever imagine.

There's an easy way to demonstrate this point. Form a group of four to eight people, and in ten minutes, come up with at least three nonobvious things you have in common. Saying you're all in the same room or the same city is too obvious. The more unusual or amusing the similarities are, the better.

I use this activity in many of my seminars, and the results are often hilarious. The things groups report as having in common range from obstreperous kids, a craving for chocolate, and a fear of flying, to the same favorite font, a dislike of furry critters, and "knowing" that broken cookies have no calories.

One group claimed that the chief characteristic they had in common was that none of them had the same first name. Another group said that none of them had ever been to the South Pole in August. A third group claimed to be wearing the same color underwear! (I resisted the urge to ask how they knew for sure.) These unpredictable, and often silly, responses are what make the exercise fun. People abandon their defenses, and zaniness takes over as they strive (quite noisily, I might add) to discover ways in which they're alike. The very process of being silly together gives them something in common.

But this is not a trivial exercise. The discovery of similarities helps not only in building new relationships, but also in repairing relationships that have gone awry. This was the case with four technical support groups to which I consulted. Their responsibilities required them to interact extensively, but their relationship was plagued by conflict. I facilitated some discussions and exercises that helped them appreciate their shared goal of delivering superior service. Then, during an activity in which I placed two of the fiercest adversaries together, I heard one of them say to the other, "You went to college there? So did I."

How the subject came up, I don't know. But suddenly, and perhaps for the first time, these two individuals saw each other not as adversaries, but as human beings, people who had lives separate from their work—lives not altogether different from their own. They suddenly realized that, for all their differences, they also had some things in common.

Did this discovery resolve all the problems between the four groups? Of course not. But it was a stepping stone. By the conclusion of our time together, the groups were not only talking to each other, they had put their heads together to identify their biggest obstacles in working together. On their own initiative, they had developed a list of steps they wanted to take to learn more about each other's work and to find ways to be more helpful to each other. Their closing comment was that they wanted to meet more often, an outcome they would have wholeheartedly rejected before our session.

This type of relationship reversal is not at all unusual when groups take the time to get to know each other better. And when they take this time early in their relationship, conflict is less likely to occur and is more likely to get resolved quickly and amicably.

What will you have in common with the next stranger you meet? Or the next customer who contacts you? Or your adversaries? It could be more than you think.

Congruent Interviewing by Audition

Gerald M. Weinberg

With the great demand for software developers these days, and with the great salaries being offered, many of my clients are having trouble sifting through the stream of supposedly qualified job applicants. People have degrees, publications, and résumés showing all sorts of job experience. But in the end, credentials aren't what counts, for software development is not an academic subject—it's a *performing* art. And that's why interviewing ultimately has to be based on performance.

Of course, not just *any* performance will do. On my SHAPE forum (a Web-based discussion group I moderate concerning the human aspects of computing), a correspondent recently wrote about how easily he gets jobs through interviews:

> I haven't been hired solely as a result of an interview for years. Here's what I do that seems to impress people with my technical skills:

1. I touch type, even the shifted number keys.
2. I can thread a half-inch reel-to-reel tape onto a tape drive with one finger. This skill has become obsolete, but has been replaced by others.
3. I know and can quickly use the keyboard equivalents of most Windows mouse commands. This is easily learned by taping a small cheat sheet to your terminal for a few weeks.
4. My attitude is relaxed; I'm pleasant to talk to.

My impression is that interviewers have made up their mind about me in the first five minutes of the interview. The rest is a formality. I think all the problems people have with interviews arise because nobody knows what to talk about after the five minutes are up. Most interviewers simply don't know enough about technical issues to talk about them for more than five minutes.

This approach is not far beyond the can-he-fog-a-mirror? performance test, though it works for this correspondent because he *does* have the technical skills for the jobs he takes. In these fast-paced days, though, not every applicant does. As a manager, how would you feel about hiring based on this "touch-type" method? And what if you're an applicant competing with people whose *only* assets are those four items? Wouldn't you like to have yourself evaluated in a better way, one that gives you a chance to display your full abilities—your *relevant* abilities?

Another correspondent wrote about how he assesses the technical competence of people who have apparently qualified résumés:

Applicants are told prior to the first interview that they'll be interviewed by an HR person, and that they'll be asked to write a short program. If somebody bills himself as a C/C++ or Visual Basic programmer, I might ask him to handwrite ten lines of simple bubble-sort code, where I give the declarations and also provide a cogent description of a bubblesort from a standard textbook.

If the applicant fails to notice that the procedures were declared incorrectly, I can legitimately assume that he probably hasn't written a lot of bug-free code lately.

This is a handwritten exercise. We thought about having people enter this program into a computer, but we felt that would only serve as a stress test and would not provide useful information.

Qualified applicants blast through this exercise in minutes and don't seem to mind this very rudimentary check. All applicants completing the exercise are immediately interviewed by an engineer. Most applicants excuse themselves, saying that they don't have the skills to write this code, and the experience is depressing for both sides—but it doesn't affect the engineers.

One part of me wonders whether this approach is unnecessarily stressful. The other part of me says that my cat could pass this test, and there's no reason to be sensitive to the feelings of people who are faking their qualifications.

For my entire career, I've advocated this kind of audition interviewing. I wrote about it in *The Psychology of Computer Programming*, and since then, several people have told me they've gotten rich building their consulting companies using such a test. I believe in checking credentials, but that's not sufficient. Would you hire an oboist for your symphony orchestra without an audition?

Be sure, though, that it's an appropriate audition for the job you're trying to fill. For instance, when hiring a designer, I wouldn't use the coding test; I would ask the person to create a rough design of something while I watch—so I can observe thought processes. I wouldn't expect a designer to know the syntax of particular languages, so I wouldn't test for that. That would be inappropriate.

It would also be inappropriate for me to observe and judge the design audition if I weren't a qualified designer myself. An audition, to be appropriate, must be conducted by those qualified to judge the performance—not merely by those appointed to manage it.

One of the people who got rich off this audition technique told me that one third of the candidates breezed through it. One third fumbled around and simply weren't qualified. But the really interesting one third took offense at the question and walked out of the interview. In fact, the question could be used partly for that specific purpose: as a simple way to exclude those who too readily take offense.

Some clients were concerned that this kind of interviewing process would create a bad reputation in the local developer community. However, a competent HR interviewer should be able to spot an applicant prone to temper tantrums and tactfully manage those people out the door—without angering them with a request that they demonstrate the ability for which they're asking to be paid. I'm not sure, however, that all HR people are that competent, and most engineers are definitely not. Over many years, none of my clients using this approach has developed a poor reputation within the developer community. On the contrary, good developers are more than happy to have a chance to distinguish themselves from the formless and clueless masses—and to do it in front of their peers.

If you fear that requiring a *written* test will spook your introverted candidates, then use a variation of this approach. Simply ask candidates to bring in some code they've written and ask them to discuss it—with other engineers, of course, not HR. If candidates get offended by this test, I doubt they're very well respected in the developer community anyway. At least not in the developer community you want to tap for candidates.

Another approach, suggested by consultant and author Naomi Karten, is to have the applicant examine and comment on code written by someone else (perhaps code prepared specifically for purposes of the interview). Part One of the test is to tell the applicant you're going to request feedback on some code, and to watch for evidence of discomfort. Part Two is to have the applicant actually review and comment on the code. The code may be extremely simple. In just a few minutes, this test can generate valuable insight into the person's skill level—and also into the honesty level of the candidate's professed qualifications. And if the job involves software maintenance, it's clearly a relevant audition.

A code-reading audition is especially appropriate if your organization uses code reviews (as every development organization should), but you must be fair to the candidates and let them know that this sample belongs to nobody in particular. Otherwise, candidates may be afraid to comment, thinking they might offend the interviewer. Of course, to participate in real technical reviews, they'll have to learn about commenting kindly while not holding back out of fear of offending the product's creator.

Like any management process, auditioning needs to be explained and sold to the participants. For this and other reasons, it needs to be kept as simple as possible, but no simpler. One of my clients tried having her engineers examine the applicant's code sample without the applicant's participation in the discussion. This worked reasonably well—except for the two applicants who slipped through by submitting code written by someone else. Since then, I've emphasized the importance of the discussion portion of the audition.

Another mistake would be to ask for more than a ten-minute audition. Believe me, you will know just about all you need to know in less than ten minutes. If you take longer, some good candidates may infer that your organization wastes engineering time on worthless activities.

It would also be a mistake if the candidate were given a deep design question and asked to give an answer in twenty-five words or less, in one minute or less. Such a test might tell the candidate more than you want to reveal about your scheduling philosophy.

Like any interviewing technique, an audition cannot be the sole criterion for selecting the candidate. For one thing, if you are known to audition using a particular problem, people will find out and prepare for that specific problem. One of my clients was well known for using the old missionaries-and-cannibals-crossing-the-river problem, and soon, slick candidates were arriving with well-rehearsed solutions.

Audition interviewing works because it is *congruent* with the position you're trying to fill. The psychologists call this quality of a test *face validity*; my consulting colleagues and I call it congruence. Either way, the test itself must clearly match the ability it's testing. It's relevant; it's open; it's honest; it's fair; and it creates an environment in which the candidates can show what they can do without playing guessing games with the interviewers.

As one of my correspondents put it, "The key is understanding whether or not they can think." To that end, almost any problem will do—as long as it's not predictable, it fits the task they're being interviewed for, and qualified people are available to observe the candidates going through their thought processes.

I believe that any thinking candidate should welcome the chance to demonstrate that he or she is, indeed, a thinking candidate.

Maneuvers to Disable a Team

Becky Winant

I f you were in the Secret Service, you would know how to kill
a president. Why? Because understanding what constitutes a
danger helps you better protect the president.

The same principle applies to teams. Teams die because no
one recognizes the warning signs of imminent disaster. In this
essay, I offer training tips for would-be project assassins. I
describe tactics that I have personally witnessed. Most can
eliminate even the best teams! Once you understand how to
carry out these destructive maneuvers, you can better identify
the ways even the best-intentioned managers may mount an
attack on your team.

1. **Add strangers to the team.** When you do this, do not
    introduce anyone. That way, team members have no
    understanding of the skills and strengths of new peo-
    ple. People will instead be judged by trivial character-
    istics instead of merit. Build awkwardness into a team
    by combining someone from the Deep South, a native
    New Yorker, and a Hawaiian—without providing intro-

ductions or holding discussions of relevant skills. Look for people with opposite hobbies or interests, so that friendships don't easily form. Add an avid sports fan to a group of people who hate organized exercise. If people tend to be timid, they may never take that step to say, "Hello, my name is Andy. What's yours?"

Advanced technique: Bring known adversaries into the group. Tell the team, "Stan is a top-notch software developer. Sally has important network experience." Pretend their skills are critical to the team. Ignore the fact that the two never come to team meetings because they want to avoid each other. The friction will affect others and will accelerate the splintering process.

2. **Restrict communication.** Talking may spark camaraderie. Remind team members that they have a job to do. Put signs around the office announcing, "QUIET, PLEASE." In fact, you might consider a team that spans Detroit, Paris, and New Delhi. Different languages and cultures can increase the likelihood of miscommunication if no translations or explanations are made. This is as good as no communication, for your purposes. If the team is based in one city, find office space on separate floors or in separate buildings. Do not publish a phone or location list. Natural inertia can work in your favor, as it will take effort for one person to find another.

   Advanced technique: Tell them the schedule is tight and e-mail is time-consuming; therefore, you will screen their messages. This way people will hesitate to send unnecessary messages.

3. **Develop a pecking order.** Only give perks to those at the top. Better equipment, window offices, time off, and invitations to elite company functions all say, "Some people are better than others." Once people see that others have special privileges, jealousy is sown.

There is a reason it's one of the seven deadly sins—it's lethal! The beauty is that, once started, animosity increases without further intervention.

4. **Expose individual faults.** Everyone has a soft spot. Find it! Choose a public forum for disclosure and make it individual. Use the person's name liberally. Also consider what approach will be most damaging— humiliation, blame, or disapproval. I have seen effective use of memos, e-mail, announcements at meetings, and rumors. If you want to blame, red ink and larger type emphasize your message. When it is hard to find faults, rumor may be a better tool. Mixing a bit of truth with something hard to refute is especially effective.

   Advanced technique: I was at one organization in which the president sent a company-wide memo blaming a new product's failure on the software team. Incredible maneuver! The president was a master assassin and the organization died shortly thereafter.

5. **Limit access to information.** If your project has a written set of requirements, you have two options: (A) Hide it—software developers are used to not having requirements, or (B) remove a third of the pages—software developers are used to obscure requirements. Also, make sure that project responsibilities are distributed, to preclude any reason for people to compare notes. Make sure that your reviews of any individual's work include seeds of doubt. For example, "That might have been important last month, but I don't think the client needs that feature now." Sometimes a simple statement, such as, "You're wrong," works wonders in reviews.

   Advanced technique: Make the team use a new, unwritten process and implement a new technology. The team may see the latter as a plus, so do not send team members to any classes or provide any time to learn. Tell them that there is no time to do so, and that besides, they are smart. This double bind will frustrate them and add stress and the probability that team spirit will crumble.

6. **Divide one team into competing groups.** This also requires splitting your project scope. You can simply create two parts with a common major interface or create slightly overlapping areas of responsibility. Give them competitive goals. Tell them, "We'll see who the better software developers are." This particular tactic will virtually eliminate information sharing. Because some people will hate this situation, individuals will resign periodically. New people will intermittently be assigned to the project—remember tactic number one! —so it will be impossible to create stability in the team or even within a group.

   Advanced technique: Divide project responsibilities—with some overlaps—between competing groups. This will secure a total lack of cooperation. This technique was originated and perfected by the U.S. government. Surely it knows what it's doing!

7. **Insist on mandatory overtime.** This will separate people from their friends and family and will add stress. Stress is an essential tool for breaking down individual commitment! When everyone is stressed, the office will be filled with irritability. Tell team members the project is very important. Tell them quality is very important. Soon, they'll really believe they have to work harder and longer to make the project a success. Taking away all vacation time helps your goal, too. Some people are sure to leave for other companies or projects. Best of all, because stress may affect quality adversely, you have the opportunity to find fault, to add a stranger with QA expertise, or to divide personnel into competing teams.

There you have my personal observations on how teams can be completely disabled. As you may notice, many techniques can be combined to accelerate the failure process. Once you begin to see how these maneuvers work, step back and resist the temptation to execute them. Like a Secret Service agent, you now have special knowledge of your enemy, knowledge that may save your next project.

How to Deal with Irate Customers

Naomi Karten

I have an affinity for penguins. They're close to the ground, and I can relate to that. But I also have a fascination with giraffes. It must be wonderful to be tall enough to eat the leaves off trees.

Being much closer to a penguin than to a giraffe in stature, I have to contend with things that taller people take for granted. For example, I'm on planes a lot, but I've never seen the overhead compartment. (I'm told I'm not missing much.) I can reach it, but just barely. I've developed a coping mechanism to deal with this, though: I simply look longingly at the compartment until a tall person offers to put my luggage up there for me. I've noticed that once these lofty individuals store my luggage for me, they always offer to take it down when we arrive.

My scanty height may be the reason a certain critter caught my attention at a zoo I once visited. There, pink as could be, were two species of flamingo. One would have had more difficulty than the other reaching the overhead compartment. The taller species, according to the sign, was called *flamingo;* the shorter species was called *lesser flamingo.*

My first reaction to these lesser flamingos was of great empathy. I could relate to their need to strain their necks to make eye contact with the taller flamingos. My second reaction, though, was one of sadness on their behalf, because their name is based on what they are relative to the taller species—not based on their intrinsic merits. You may laugh, but how would you like to go through life as a lesser flamingo? That could very well affect how you view yourself, and it could certainly affect how others view you (other flamingos, at least).

What something is called—whether it's a living critter or a thing or a concept—affects perceptions and attitudes. And these perceptions and attitudes sometimes have unintended consequences. This is certainly true when you serve or support customers. For example, once you label someone as a "difficult customer," you are more likely to see that person as difficult and to react accordingly, rather than to seek ways of working successfully with that person.

When managers ask me for advice about helping their staffs deal with irate customers, my first suggestion is to banish the word "irate" from their vocabularies. Sure, customers sometimes erupt with anger, hostility, and vehement vocalizations. But the term "irate" somehow suggests customers who are second-class citizens, people who are a nuisance, an irritation, or an interruption—even though their grievances may be as valid and worthy of your attention as all the others to which you respond. In fact, these customers may have become angry because their problems were deemed *unworthy* of your attention in the first place.

Add to "irate customer" other designations I often hear, such as resistant customer, problem customer, demanding customer, or unreasonable customer. Once you characterize people with labels like these, you may become less inclined to try to understand the causes of their behavior—causes that might reasonably drive anyone (even you) to react in exactly the same way. You may respond to your so-called problem customers in a defensive, get-rid-of-'em manner—even when they approach you with a soft-spoken, meek, and mellow manner.

Notice how you characterize your customers—and all others, for that matter—when their attitude or behavior differs from what you'd like it to be. It could be that your characterizations say more about you than about them. On behalf of myself and lesser flamingos everywhere—as well as of dachshunds and midget giraffes—think twice about the labels you apply. That's the tall and short of it.

Part Three:
Mastering Projects

Projects are team efforts aimed at bringing something new into the world, which makes them sensitive measures of our individual and team effectiveness. To paraphrase an ancient Chinese proverb, managing a large project is like boiling a small fish—a delicate job. Rick Brenner leads off this section with some small delicacies of his own: poetry that mirrors the sensitivity of projects with a delicacy of observation. Johanna Rothman then transforms some of Rick's haiku into more hearty fare—recognizing the significance of slips and gleaning information on how to master them.

Brian Pioreck neatly connects his personal effectiveness with the outcomes of the projects he works on, even when they're supposedly simple efforts—such as making a pancake breakfast. Marie Benesh scales up Brian's insights, teaching us how to recognize and manage some of the common pitfalls of gargantuan projects, those that are more like banquets than breakfasts. To conclude the section, Eileen Strider shows us how to recognize and cope with projects that have eluded our mastery and become indigestible.

Ten Project Haiku

Rick Brenner

I
Our project was late,
so we added more people.
The problem got worse.

II
When requirements changed,
the schedule did not—were we
headed for trouble?

III
We were doing fine,
'til they reduced the budget.
Now we're overspent.

IV
We think about risks.
We have contingency plans.
Oops . . . but not for that.

V
I gave estimates.
They cut all of them in half.
Next time I'll pad them.

VI
We can't get it right
and still come in on schedule.
Why can't we do both?

VII
We hired consultants
who told us how to fix things.
They don't understand.

VIII
There is no more time,
but the work is unfinished.
Take more time from Test.

IX
The module failed test,
so first we changed all the tests.
Now, the requirements.

X
If a project fails
but we keep working on it,
has it really failed?

It's Just the First Slip

Johanna Rothman

recently read an article by a well-known author. He claimed that your first project slip isn't so bad; the third or fourth project slips are the bad ones.

Right away, red flags went up in my mind. I completely disagreed with his conclusion.

The first slip is your initial indication that something is wrong. Don't believe that you can make up time in your project. You can't. At the first slip, you should take a step back and observe what's going on—versus what you'd like to have going on. By the time you hit the third or fourth slip, you've already lost the schedule battle.

When software projects start to fall behind, they're talking to you, the project manager. The first slip is a whisper: "Your expectation is not matching my reality. Listen to me. I can tell you my reality." If you ignore the first slip, the second one is a murmur: "Things aren't quite right. Don't you want to know what's happening?"

At the third slip, the project says: "Knock-knock. Are you there? Don't you care about what's going on?" At the fourth, the project yells: "Hey, you! You didn't listen to me when you could have taken action. You'll pay for this."

I prefer to have projects whisper to me. (Otherwise, people think I'm crazy when I yell back at my projects.) If you and your project agree on reality at early stages, you can make small adjustments with big results.

I recently worked with a company as it prepared to ship a Beta release. The developers were having trouble getting the software ready in time for the scheduled Beta date.

I was ready with questions about the schedule, the defective data, the testing, and the way the code was integrated. Luckily, I asked about schedule first.

"Oh, we planned the schedule six months ago," they said. "We haven't changed it."

I asked if they had met their milestone dates.

"Well, not really. We missed the first deadline. The requirements weren't done, but we had to get started, so we began designing without knowing all the requirements."

This is risky, but not a terrible thing, especially if they planned to manage the risks. I asked about the other milestones.

"Well, since the requirements weren't done, we couldn't finish the design on time. Since the design wasn't done, the coding was a little late." The first slip cascaded into slips for every other milestone.

Then I asked what turned out to be the key question: "When did the testers know what to test, if the requirements, design, and implementation were a little late?" The answer I got was, "Last week."

Uh-oh. I asked one more question: "How much testing did you plan for this project?" They looked at each other and said, "Oh, we planned to do about six weeks' worth, but I guess we won't get to that now, will we?"

Let me emphasize that these people were not stupid. They had a simple problem with a huge, cascading effect: The first slip led to more slips. Then they had trouble facing the reality of their project. They started with a small slip, but because they kept going, the small slip magnified the effect of subsequent slips.

If the developers had stopped at the first slip and rethought their work or replanned the schedule, they might have been able to meet their target Beta date. Now, as I explained to them before we rolled up our sleeves to finish the testing, their only option was to extend the schedule.

Slips tell you valuable information about your project. Something is not going according to plan. Before that something turns into lots of things, have a heart-to-heart discussion with your project.

Quality Begins at Home

Brian Pioreck

The patterns of behavior woven into our lives are difficult to recognize, so we sometimes miss opportunities to use our strengths and to review our less-developed talents. This revelation became crystal clear to me a few years ago, on my wife's birthday, and at the same time, it exposed a lucrative business opportunity.

That year, Melissa's birthday fell on a Saturday. Because my job as a consultant requires extensive travel, the fact that I would be home that day made it even more of a holiday. Mel wanted breakfast in bed—buttermilk pancakes from scratch, bacon, and orange juice. This kind of breakfast happens to be a specialty of mine, so I readily agreed.

There was just one complication: Mel's and my infant son, Zachary, who was just fifteen months old at the time. If you have children, you know that between the ages of birth and about three years old, they rule the household. Zachary was running our lives. Our other children, Rebecca and Anna, were older (thirteen and six, respectively) and were somewhat more able to help prepare the birthday breakfast.

I arrived home on Friday night and made my first mistake: I failed to build infrastructure. The kitchen was cluttered with dinner dishes, but Rebecca, who is normally responsible for these, accepted a last-minute sleepover invitation with my approval. I decided to clean the kitchen in the morning. First, I needed to decompress from a week of work and travel. There was a game on television, and I played with the kids with it on in the background. When bedtime arrived, I made a mental note to wake earlier to deal with the mess.

Between my compensating for Zachary's developing survival skills and cleaning the kitchen, Saturday morning was a farce. By mid-morning, nary an egg had been cracked. So, I went to the bedroom to renegotiate the breakfast delivery time with my wife. Luckily, I had gifts and flowers to soften the blow. I contracted breakfast out to the Country Café.

Sunday dawned with new promise, but I had traded one failed illusion for another. I had thought, incorrectly, that the dishes were the crux of Saturday's problems, and now I realized that I had renegotiated a due date with little more than good intentions. I still had prepared nothing.

My staff was a problem. Anna, my six-year-old, was full of enthusiasm but lacked most of the needed skills. Rebecca, my teenager, had most of the appropriate skills but lacked patience with her peers. And Zachary! Just keeping him from bringing the whole operation to a halt would require my complete attention.

Beyond my personal issues, I had underestimated the complexities of my deliverable: a from-scratch, homemade, in-bed breakfast. The Country Café was not an option today. Time was ticking. The girls were arguing—Becky wanted Anna to mix the ingredients as Becky added them to the bowl. Anna objected—there is no growth in mixing. Anna wanted to sift flour. Anna wanted to break the eggs.

Zachary was pulling sections out of the Sunday paper and spreading them on our bedroom floor. While retrieving him, I gave Melissa a look that said, "I have run out of parenting tools. I need help."

From over the edge of the newspaper, she gave me a look that said, "You're the big-time consultant—*you* figure it out." I briefly allowed myself a vision of going out for a quart of milk and coming back in twenty-five years.

That's when I saw the connection between pancakes and software. The acts of organizing a breakfast and managing application development became a common vision. That weekend I suffered from the same kind of blind spots and unverified assumptions that I have spent years helping my clients avoid. If I couldn't coordinate my kids' efforts, how could I expect to coordinate software projects? This was no longer a matter of fulfilling a birthday wish. This was a challenge to my professional credibility.

My friend Sam Bayer, a successful software entrepreneur, says that every project must have three things to succeed. First, you must have a goal that is achievable, measurable, and easy to describe. Second, you must have a committed team. Third, you must realize that the project is a journey. How you travel toward your goal is just as important as reaching it.

We had our goal: a delicious pancake and bacon breakfast delivered in close proximity to Melissa's birthday, a good time, and no tears among the staff. When managing a project, do you have the goal clearly in mind? A project can spin out many deliverables. Which are the ones that will make yours a success? Is the goal achievable and can the team you assembled achieve it? You need to have a reasonable expectation of this when you start, plus a contingency plan ready if expectations outpace reality.

Melissa, in her wisdom, has instilled a saying into our family culture that I used to motivate the girls: "When Mamma ain't happy, ain't nobody happy." This, our grumbling stomachs, and a desire to deliver on her birthday wish solidified our commitment.

For the projects you manage, how do you generate the commitments needed to complete them successfully? Why should everyone pull together? Hint: It's not for the paycheck.

Think back to projects you loved being part of. What was special about those efforts? Perhaps it was a feeling of camaraderie bordering on family. Maybe the usual company red tape was cast aside or the right thing happened just when it was needed. Whatever the circumstances, I'd be willing to bet that the special part was more than completing the project on time and on budget. We take something we cherish with us from loved projects, and we seek to experience it again. Those projects change us and are worth at least as much as—if not more than—the deliverables themselves.

The girls and I marshaled our resources. I held Zachary and guided the girls through the recipe. Becky showed Anna how to measure a level cup of flour. While Anna did the other cups, Becky got the bacon going and measured the rest of the dry ingredients. Anna sifted, and everyone got to break eggs (though we had to fish the eggshell out of Zachary's cracked contribution). Everyone even got to flip pancakes. Breakfast was delivered before noon, with giggles and hugs, and was enjoyed by all. While cleaning up, worn-out from the morning, I pondered my wrinkled hands and considered that most processes have room for improvement.

Perhaps you are looking for your next professional challenge. If you are a project manager or team leader struggling with quality deliverables, I'd like to help. I am offering an invaluable three-day workshop on making projects work, plus all the pancakes you can eat. Just remember you have to make enough for everybody, and everybody should find a way to help. The third day is for cleaning, and you'll need some rubber gloves. But it's worth the effort. You just might make something you'll cherish long after the pancakes are gone.

Managing Your ERP: How to Avoid Common Pitfalls of Implementation

Marie Benesh

Many organizations have undertaken enterprise-wide initiatives to replace legacy systems, to install enterprise resource planning products (ERP)—such as SAP and PeopleSoft—and to redesign business processes. Some were driven to these initiatives in the 1990's by Y2K concerns, others by a desire to enable growth and enhance their information management capabilities.

I have found four areas where ERP projects are most vulnerable, and in fact these problem areas have affected every project I have worked on in my career:

- managing communication
- facilitating the decision-making process
- testing and managing your infrastructure
- living with your ERP

The successes and failures from projects of the past contain lessons that can make your ERP projects successful. In this essay, I address each of these areas and offer some key insights for successfully implementing and integrating an ERP into your environment.

Managing Communication

Your ERP project will most likely be one of the largest projects you have undertaken. It may include anywhere from 100 to 300 or more team members, including functional leaders and user-test personnel. When you are working with that many people, a key area to focus on is how you are going to communicate across all the teams and with all these people.

If you are going to succeed, then someone, perhaps you, must take the leadership role in providing tools and processes for managing communication. Communication processes must span multiple teams—across technical and functional areas. From vision and requirements planning to the functional implementation and rollout, communication is an essential part of overall productivity and effectiveness.

I have found that a central repository structure is especially effective when it is designed to be accessible to all project members—from senior management to outside vendors. It may be a Web-based repository, a Lotus Notes application, or an application built in MS Exchange and Visual Basic. It typically includes vision and goals, project timelines, issue management, change-control management, requirements documentation (with revisions), project tracking, and status reporting. Functions such as indexing and the ability to view information in different ways make finding information easy for everyone. Workflow features further enhance the management processes by alerting key individuals of changes or the need for approvals.

To succeed with a repository like this, be prepared to assign someone to build and maintain it. As the repository is used, people will think of better ways to organize it and new sections to add. Be sure that the repository is updated and modified to meet the needs of those who you expect will use it. It will be well worth the development cost.

Facilitating the Decision-Making Process

Another aspect of implementing an ERP is decision-making: securing decisions and making them stick. As integrated products are implemented, decisions made in one functional area can impact the design of another functional area or the plans of the technical team. In order to ensure success and eliminate rework, decisions need to be made and understood across teams.

In most of the teams I have worked with, cross-team decision-making is the most difficult cultural change to make. It requires communication with the right people and a formal decision-making process.

The first question to ask is, "Who can make what kind of decisions?" If a decision involves only programming issues or a change in the development process, you may only need to contact a development manager and any stakeholders, such as test leads and application leads, who may be directly affected by the decision. But if a decision involves changing a policy or a business process, you need to know who can make this change and make it stick. Is it the manager of a functional area like Accounting, or does the decision need to be made by the VP of Finance? Who is affected by the decision and does the decision-maker know?

Clarify who the key decision-makers are in advance. Use a list that might say, for example, that all policy decisions for Finance must be made by the VP, and all operational decisions for Finance can be made by the manager of Finance.

The decision-making process must provide the key decision-makers and other stakeholders with enough information—of the kind they'll require to make an informed decision. All of this information should be provided in writing so they can look at it, review it, and ask further questions. The documentation should include the following elements:

- a brief description of the decision that needs to be made and the options available

- a list of potential impacts for each option
- a statement of costs associated with each option
- an estimate of project delays associated with each option

Finally, decision-makers need to know when decisions must be made, in order to avoid delaying the project schedule. Many times, people have all the information but just don't realize the impact a delay will have, and so they may hold a decision, pondering it, checking with others for opinions. Given a deadline, most people will turn around a decision in time. Without that knowledge, decision-makers may not perceive any urgency to make the decision at all.

Placing the right information in the hands of the right people makes decision-making simpler and streamlined, and it reduces rumor and speculation regarding potential changes to the project or system.

Testing and Managing Your Infrastructure

The IT team can greatly improve the chances for ERP success by following a rigorous testing process that employs the industry's best practices. People often think of testing only in terms of business processes, asking questions such as, "Can I run transactions and get back the information I want?" In the days of the mainframe, or in single-server or departmental environments, testing only in terms of the business process was quite often enough. Systems were "one box, one connection."

Today, with client/server technology, we have an enormously complex technical environment to manage. For the ERP testing group, testing takes on a new meaning. Every support process (like backup and restore), and every interface, server, desktop, and network component must be tested individually and then end-to-end. You've got to test for stability and reliability, and you have to test the ability to deploy across your enterprise, on any and all platforms you choose for your servers and desktop.

Often, your environment will already consist of mixes of platforms, particularly on the desktop. The variety of applications used in desktop projects establishes a mix of configurations and setups in your environment. To streamline your ERP configurations and to have them work consistently, standards should be developed and adhered to for each product, especially on the desktop.

The desktop arena can be the most difficult to manage. Users are used to having their workstations set up their own way, and often this lack of standardization can be a huge challenge to the ERP project. Establishing desktop standards may make sense to you, but it won't to your users. Be prepared to help them understand why standardization is necessary and how you will try to support their needs—short of adding cost to the project's bottom line.

Because the client/server arena is highly configurable, the ERP teams will need to send small groups of technologists to each geographic location to assess the environment, make recommendations, and establish technical training plans for local support. They must later return to reinspect for adequate compliance. This assessment process may require a change not only in your process, but also in your culture.

The costs of noncompliance and the instability of a nonstandard, highly complex technical environment can make testing your worst nightmare. A failure to manage this complexity can be too much for the project to bear and will likely reduce the overall benefit of implementing an integrated enterprise system.

Living with Your ERP

Following is a comment often heard on large ERP projects: "I can't wait until this project is over and we can get back to the way things were."

But the truth is, things will not go back to the way they were before your ERP went live. One profound lesson that I've seen clients learn again and again is that ERP brings a permanent and fundamental change in how they do business and in how they support the business through information technology. Many of the team structures put in place to deliver the ERP will need to remain in place to support it, although on a smaller scale.

You will always need to manage the integration of your ERP, so your planning team will remain a necessary part of ongoing operations. Communication will still need to occur across a large part of your organization, so your repository will need to be maintained and your communication processes will need to remain in place. Your decision-making process will be exercised with every significant change and every upgrade of your ERP. And your infrastructure testing will be challenged with each new release of your ERP, as technologies are added to enhance the capabilities of the product.

Most importantly, you will have attained a new level of process maturity as a result of this implementation. You may find that other projects seem to go more smoothly, benefiting from what you've learned about managing communication and decision-making. Surprises will occur less often because you will have learned to plan with integration in mind. Your development methods and processes will be more effective, and it will make sense to spread this value to other teams and projects in the company.

If you are in the beginning stages of your ERP implementation, know that this will be a difficult journey. But this may also be an opportunity to implement the processes you've always wished you could implement. You may now have a chance to introduce some of the rigor you knew was needed on other, smaller projects, but which you couldn't muster before, for lack of management support. Best of all, you can turn this into an opportunity for growth, and you may even have fun in the process.

Recognizing Runaway Projects

Eileen Strider

I remember the first time I saw the comedy classic *Monty Python and the Holy Grail*, especially the scene in which a farcical version of King Arthur abandons a battle (in this case, against a ferocious rabbit) and orders his knights to "Run away, run away!" When I realize a project is in trouble, this is definitely my first thought. How about you? Even if you haven't seen this movie, do you recognize the urge to drop everything and retreat?

In this essay, I describe projects that not only make you want to run away but are running away themselves. If you have never experienced a runaway project—or perhaps never knew how to tell that a project was out of control—you'll learn how to recognize a runaway when one eventually comes your way. If you believe you're already working on a runaway project—and suspect you're losing your mind!—you'll find some ways to regain control of your project and your sanity.

For our purposes, we can define a runaway project as one in which all or part of the project is moving in a direction that takes you *farther from your goal rather than closer to it.*

Typically, this means that some or all of a project is out of control. Here are some symptoms of projects that have become runaways:

1. The scope of requirements keeps changing or growing. Perhaps no one knows what the real requirements are or *whose* requirements they are.
2. Customers are running away from the project. For example, they don't show up for status meetings; they stop asking when the project will be finished; or they threaten to cancel the project.
3. Competition is driving customers away from your products.
4. Employees are running away from the project by asking for transfers or quitting altogether.
5. Design additions or modifications are accumulating relentlessly.
6. The project is behind schedule and over budget, and people have little confidence in the estimates to completion.
7. Supported configurations are growing boundlessly.
8. You're not sure what goal the project is trying to reach.
9. In the worst case, no one really knows *who* is responsible for ensuring that the project is managed and under control. Someone may have the title of project manager, but does that person have sole responsibility for management and control?

As you read this list of symptoms, you may have wondered how anyone could let a project get so out of control. Well, I know that runaways happen regularly, and most shops are not immune to these symptoms—somehow, they sneak up on us.

If you are the project manager, you may believe that the project is being managed. You may acknowledge that from time to time there are problems, but you convince yourself that your corrective actions put everything back on track. Nothing that you can see is obviously wrong, and you're too busy to look more closely. Still, you have this slight nagging feeling—in the pit of your stomach or in the farthest corner of your mind—and this slight feeling is the surest sign of a runaway project.

The cause of this feeling isn't anything specific—you just hear a tiny voice whispering that *something just doesn't seem right*. Of course, you think you may just be imagining this voice or feeling. You're not even sure it's about this project. Maybe you're distracted, or your stomach is just acting up. Since no one else is saying anything, it must not be real. You pray it's not real, because if it is real, you'll have to do something about it. Sometimes, the thought of saying out loud what you're feeling is just too scary.

Recognition is the biggest and most difficult step toward regaining control of a runaway project. So, if you recognize you have a runaway project, give yourself an appreciation. Find people with whom you feel safe discussing the project, and ask for their support. Talking to someone about what you're thinking and feeling can bring you great relief. From there, muster your courage to act. As a former CIO, I know this is no small feat. Your ability to recognize a problem and to ask for support calls on your leadership skills, what consultant and author Jerry Weinberg refers to as "the ability to act appropriately in difficult interpersonal situations, even though you may be confused, angry, or so afraid you want to run away and hide." Like the Cowardly Lion—in another great movie, the *Wizard of Oz*—we all have to find our courage. In the midst of a runaway project, you must find it.

Having found your courage, you have a choice of actions:

1. Regain control of what has been out of control and proceed with the project.
2. Stop the project, salvage what you can, and begin again, applying what you have learned.
3. Reevaluate the need for the project.
4. Seek outside help to assess the project and to help correct the problems.

5. If no one will heed your advice, *run away* before it's fatal. By helping yourself first, you may later be able to help others.

The actions you take will not necessarily be easy, and others may fail to see the wisdom and courage of your actions. However, you will feel more confident once you address the symptoms of a runaway project and make a decision—even if it means running away yourself, like King Arthur and his knights—to regain control of the situation, starting with your courage to act.

Part Four:
Changing the
Organization

Once we have succeeded in demonstrating our effectiveness by successfully completing a project or two, our aspirations naturally turn to helping others do the same. But change is not the simple linear process that we might hope, as Steve Smith explains in his essay on Virginia Satir's Change Model. To change an organization, we need tools to aid our systems thinking, and that's just what Esther Derby gives us in her essay on modeling organizational change. Pat Medvick then describes the sort of organizational change needed to create a process for the development of useful scientific software, and James Bach shows us how the search for better practices is not a mere intellectual exercise, but more of a real-life adventure.

The Satir Change Model

Steven M. Smith

mprovement is always possible. This conviction is at the heart of the transformation system developed by family therapist Virginia Satir. Her system helps people to improve their lives by transforming the way they see and express themselves.

The Satir System features a five-stage Change Model that describes the effects each stage has on feelings, thinking, performance, and physiology (see Figure 1). Using the principles embodied in this model, you can improve how you process change and how you help others process change. In this paper, I summarize the characteristics of each stage to provide an overview of the Change Model.

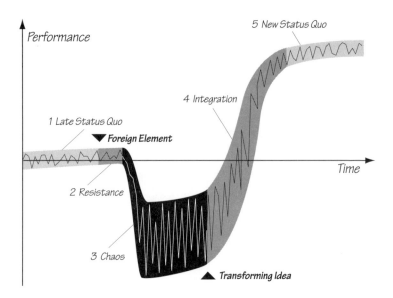

Figure 1: *The impact on group performance of a well-assimilated change during the five stages of the Satir Change Model.*

Stage 1: Late Status Quo

At this stage, the group is at a familiar place. The performance pattern is consistent. Stable relationships give members a sense of belonging and identity. People know what to expect, how to react, and how to behave.

Implicit and explicit rules underlie people's behavior. Members of a group at this stage attach survival value to the rules, even if the rules may be harmful. For instance, the chief of an engineering group has an explicit rule—all projects must be completed on schedule. When the flu halts the work of several engineers, the chief requires the group to compensate by working ten hours per day, seven days per week. After experiencing too many crises at both work and home, the engineers begin to bicker and the project falls apart.

For this group, the chief's explicit rule about deadlines is characterized by their Late Status Quo. They don't necessarily enjoy the amount of work they have to do, but they know and understand what is expected of them. The team feels the pressure from the chief's rule about deadlines and compensates accordingly. The pressure works for small problems. With a major problem like the flu, the group cannot cope with the chief's expectations and a pattern of dysfunctional behavior starts.

Poor communication is a symptom of a dysfunctional group. Members use blaming, placating, and other *incongruent* communication styles to cope with feelings like anger and guilt. Stress may lead to physical symptoms, such as headaches and gastrointestinal pain, which may increase absenteeism.

Caught in a web of dysfunctional behaviors, the people whose opinions count the most—whether they are managers or others in the group—are unaware of the imbalance between the group and its environment. However, new information and concepts from outside the group can make members more aware of the possibility of improvement.

Stage 2: Resistance

In this stage, the group confronts a *foreign element* that requires a response. Often imported by a small minority seeking change, this element brings the most influential individuals in the group face-to-face with a crucial issue.

A foreign element threatens the stability of familiar power structures. Most members resist it by denying its validity, avoiding the issue, or blaming someone for causing the problem. These blocking tactics are accompanied by unconscious physical responses, such as shallow breathing and closed posture.

Resistance clogs awareness and conceals the desires highlighted by the foreign element. For example, a powerful minority within the marketing department of a tool manufacturer engages a consultant to do a market survey. She finds a disturbing trend: A growing number of clients believe that a competitor is producing superior-quality products at a lower price. Middle and upper management vehemently deny the findings and dispute the validity of the survey methods. But after a series of frank discussions with key clients, upper management accepts the findings. The managers develop a vision for propelling the company into a leadership position in the industry for its product quality and support.

People in this stage need help opening up, becoming aware, and overcoming the urge to deny, avoid, or blame.

Stage 3: Chaos

In this stage, the group enters the unknown. Relationships shatter: Old expectations may no longer be valid; old reactions may cease to be effective; and old behaviors may not be possible.

The loss of belonging and identity triggers anxiety and vulnerability. On a physical level, these feelings may even set off nervous disorders, such as shaking, dizziness, tics, and rashes. Members may behave uncharacteristically by reverting to childhood survival rules in an effort to find stability. For instance, a manufacturing company cancels the development of a major new product, reduces the number of employees, and reorganizes. Many of the surviving employees lose their ability to concentrate for much of the day. Desperately seeking new relationships that offer hope, the employees search for new jobs. Both manufacturing yield and product quality take a nosedive.

Managers of groups experiencing Chaos should expect group performance to plummet during this stage. Until individuals accept the foreign element, they form only halfhearted relationships with each other. Erratic performance in the Chaos stage mirrors the members' search for a beneficial relationship to the foreign element.

In Chaos, all people need help focusing on their feelings, acknowledging their fear, and using their support systems. Management needs special help avoiding any attempt to short-circuit this stage with magical solutions. The Chaos stage is vital to the transformation process.

Stage 4: Integration

During this stage, the members discover a *transforming idea* that shows how the foreign element can benefit them. The group becomes excited. New relationships emerge and offer the opportunity for identity and belonging. With practice, performance improves rapidly.

For example, an experienced accounting group must convert to a new computer system. The group resists the new system, fearing it will turn them into novices. But group members eventually discover that proficiency in operating this widely used system increases their value in the marketplace. Believing that the change may lead to salary increases or better jobs, the members begin a vigorous conversion to the new system.

Awareness of new possibilities enables authorship of new rules that encourage appropriate and congruent reactions, expectations, and behaviors. People may feel euphoric and invincible, as the transforming idea may be so powerful that it becomes a panacea.

Members in this stage need more support than might be expected, especially if they become frustrated when things fail to work perfectly on the first try. Although people feel good during Integration, they are afraid that any transformation may suddenly evaporate, disconnecting them from their new relationships and plunging them back into Chaos. The members need reassurance and help finding new methods for coping with difficulties.

Stage 5: New Status Quo

If the change is well conceived and assimilated, the group and its environment enter the New Status Quo stage and are in better accord. Performance stabilizes at a higher level than in the Late Status Quo stage.

The group is healthy, calm, and alert. People are now centered emotionally and physically, as is evident in their improved posture and deeper breathing. They feel free to observe and communicate what is really happening. A sense of accomplishment and possibility permeates the atmosphere.

In this stage, the members still need to feel safe so they can practice and experiment with new solutions. Everyone—manager and members—needs to encourage each other to continue exploring the imbalances between the group and its environment and to further reduce the resistance to change.

I've observed groups that, after many change cycles, become *learning organizations*—they learn how to cope with change. The people in these organizations are no longer threatened or anxious about the same situations that they used to experience as foreign elements. Now, these situations excite and motivate them.

For example, the customer services group of a computer manufacturer learns to adapt its repair policies and techniques to any new product. Supporting a new computer system used to scare the group, but not anymore. Management communicates and reinforces the vision of seamless support of new products. Some members influence the design of support features for the new products. Other members plan and teach training courses. Everyone provides feedback to improve the process.

Postscript: Coping With Change

Virginia Satir's Change Model describes the change patterns she saw during therapy sessions with families. In my experience, the patterns she describes occur with any group of people that is confronted by change.

I use this model to identify ways to help a group make a successful transformation from a Late Status Quo to a New Status Quo. Table 1 summarizes my suggestions on how to help during each stage of the Change Model.

Table 1: *Actions for each stage that will help a group change more quickly and effectively.*

Stage	Description	How to Help
1	Late Status Quo	Encourage people to seek improvement, information, and concepts from outside the group.
2	Resistance	Help people to open up, become aware, and overcome the urge to react with denial, avoidance, or blame.
3	Chaos	Help build a safe environment that enables people to focus on their feelings, acknowledge their fear, and use their support systems. Help management to avoid any attempt to short-circuit this stage with magical solutions.
4	Integration	Offer reassurance and help in finding new methods for coping with difficulties.
5	New Status Quo	Help people feel safe so they can practice what they've learned during the change process.

The actions in Table 1 will help people cope. Actions that inhibit coping and resist the fundamental foreign element of change will retard an organization's ability to make core changes. But organizations that create a safe environment where people are encouraged to cope will increase their capacity for change and will more effectively respond to whatever challenges are thrown their way.

References

Satir, Virginia, et al. *The Satir Model: Family Therapy and Beyond.* Palo Alto, Calif.: Science and Behavior Books, 1991.

Weinberg, Gerald M., *Quality Software Management, Volume 4: Anticipating Change.* New York: Dorset House Publishing, 1997.

Modeling Organizational Change

Esther Derby

When you confront a problem that exists in the way your work group functions, you're implementing an organizational change. By taking a critical look at your process and using some theories from organizational design, you can fix the problem—and improve your organization's ability to deliver high-quality results.

I'm writing for managers responsible for quality—QA, test, or development group managers—so I'm going to assume that you work in that capacity. You may feel skeptical about organizational change; that it's something that happens to you, not something you do as part of your job. It's true, you probably don't have control over many of the elements that go into an organizational design, such as compensation or overall structure, but in your career, you will be involved in making thousands of small-scale organizational changes. That's why a familiarity with the theories and techniques used in large-scale organizational change can be of benefit to you as a professional.

Organizational change is a transformation made to a complex system. This is true whether you are changing an entire company or making adjustments within your project or work group. As a manager, you change the system every time you make a course correction within your span of control.

Systems, even small ones, are very complex. They comprise many variables, and the relationships among them are not simple: Any one variable may be influenced by a host of factors. Moreover, any action can affect more than one variable in the system. Your job in designing an organizational change is to understand the interplay of factors and to identify ways to guide the system in the direction you desire.

Circular Causation

Let's look at an example that I've worked with, one that is probably familiar to you.

In this case, a software development organization released an application with several major defects. The customers were unhappy and asked for a special release to fix the problems. Management then agreed to do the "special" without delaying the schedule for the next feature release.

Predictably enough, under the pressure of putting out a problem-fix release in addition to the regular release, the testing staff cut some corners, and more defects went out with the regular release.

In terms of cause and effect, this sequence of events looks like this:

> Request for special release➜ greater workload➜ more pressure to deliver➜ corners cut in testing➜ more defects released➜ request for special release

Notice that the last effect is the same as the first. So, instead of fixing the problem (that the customers are unhappy with the number of defects), the choice to put out a special release has perpetuated the problem. This is circular causation. Identifying the best place in the circle to make a correction can be difficult.

In project work, we tend to think in terms of simple cause and effect: The build is three weeks behind schedule, therefore testing will begin three weeks behind schedule. But circular causation is much more common, especially in complex systems. A simple cause and effect may in fact have a cause of its own, and these causation loops are subtle. A model of the system helps you see the complexity and lets you play out several options before you commit to a particular action.

Corrective Action

The easiest kind of model to develop is a simple diagram of effects. To model a system, you need to identify the *measurable* events within it. The measurements don't have to be exact, but they do have to be based on observable evidence of the events in the system.

Figure 1 shows a simple model of the system that is operating in the organization described above, as too many defects are released with its product.

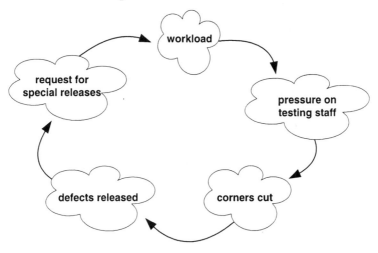

Figure 1. The current state: The customer is dissatisfied with the number of defects in the current release and requests a special release (in addition to the already scheduled feature release) to correct problems. The workload goes up, which puts more pressure on the testing staff. The testing staff reacts to the pressure by cutting corners, which leads to more defects released . . . which leads to another request for a special "bug fix" release.

The clouds represent effects you can observe in the system. The arrows indicate that, as one effect increases, so does the one pointed to by the arrow. As the workload gets bigger, pressure on the testing staff increases, and so on.

It's easy to see the loop here. Now that the circular causality is clear, we can envision an intervention that will stabilize the system and bring the defect rate down.

First, look for an activity to "do more of." This is the simplest organizational intervention. You can't always find this kind of lever, but it's worth the search. In our example, however, we clearly do not want to increase any of these effects.

If you fail to find a natural lever, generate several ideas for reducing some of the negative effects. Try to come up with at least three options (in many cases, you can come up with more). They don't have to be perfect options; they just have to be options. In fact, looking for the ideal correction is a common mistake that keeps managers from taking a "good enough" action that would correct a problem sooner.

So, in our example, what are some options?

- Add more testers.
- Require overtime for the testing staff.
- Implement a change-management process that examines trade-offs and allows management to review priorities and negotiate with the customers.

Adding resources or mandating overtime are common interventions for all sorts of problems. Option three—changing the process to manage the workload—is common in some organizations and unknown in others.

How will each of these interventions impact the existing system? In the following sections, I review the effects of each of these options.

Option 1: Add More Testers

Suppose you can hire testers who are fully productive the first week on the job. By distributing the test cases among all the testers, you reduce the workload for each tester, reduce pressure, and break the cycle of increased defects.

Sounds good. But even if the new testers are up to speed on the first day, adding staff requires more effort to coordinate tasks and communication, and this increases the workload. Figure 2 shows the impact of adding testers who don't have any learning curve. The existing testers will have to absorb the additional effort of coordination and communication, and this cancels out any benefit derived from reducing the number of test cases each tester is assigned.

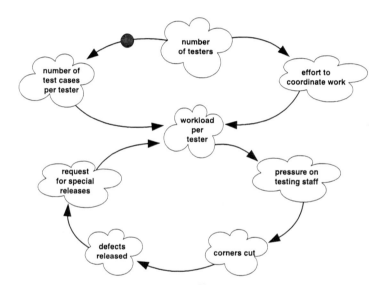

Figure 2. Management responds to the request for a special release by adding more testers: If new testers are able to contribute immediately, and they don't require time from the experienced testers for coaching and answering questions, the workload on each tester will be reduced. (The black dot indicates that as one effect goes up, the other goes down, and vice versa.) There will be another effect of adding more testers: additional effort to coordinate the work. The additional effort will most likely cancel out the benefits of each tester having responsibility for fewer test cases.

In most cases, though, you probably won't find testers who can be fully productive without some coaching and support from experienced staff. The experienced testers will have to spend time orienting the new testers and answering their questions, which increases both their workload and the amount of pressure they experience.

Figure 3 shows how the system looks with the addition of testers who need information and coaching from existing staff. This follows the conventional wisdom that adding staff late in a project actually slows progress.

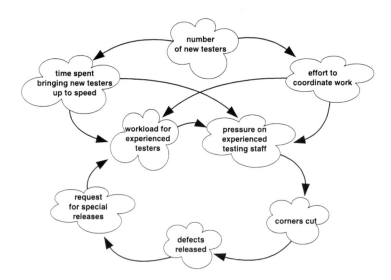

Figure 3. Management responds to the request for a special release by adding more testers: The new testers need to ask questions and get coaching from the experienced testers in order to be productive. In addition to increased effort to coordinate work, experienced staff need to spend time with the new testers, reducing the amount of time they can spend on their own testing tasks. This outcome is the most likely, unless management actively works to manage the impact of adding staff.

While beefing up the testing staff may be an excellent long-term strategy, in the near term, it will increase the stress on the system and perpetuate the problem. The organization in our example may still choose this option, but it will need to take additional actions to prevent the system from spinning out of control.

Option 2: Required Overtime

Required overtime is common in our industry. We've all been on projects where 50- to 60-hour weeks are the norm during a crunch. Most people can put up with it for a short period of time and continue to function, although less effectively. Many people tolerate long stretches of overtime because they have stock options or some other financial interest in the company. The intention of overtime is to allocate more time to tasks and therefore reduce the need to cut corners. The reality is that efficiency decreases when people work overtime, and the intended benefits of the extra hours are seldom realized.

What happens when overtime continues for an extended period and morale starts to diminish? Testers become de-motivated—and more corners get cut. They may even start to leave, increasing the workload *and* pressure put on those who remain (Figure 4).

If the developers are also subject to required overtime, they may introduce more errors as they attempt to correct the defects found in testing. This leads to more defects, more requests for special releases, greater workload, and so on, throughout the cycle shown in Figure 4.

As with Option 1, we've added complexity to the system, while keeping the problem going and probably making it worse.

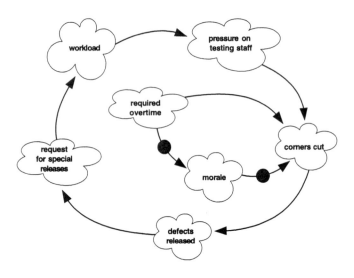

Figure 4. Management responds to the request for a special release by instituting required overtime to meet the current feature release and still accommodate the special release: Mandatory overtime leads to a drop in morale and more pressure on the testers. The drop in morale causes the testers to cut more corners because they feel the situation is hopeless, which leads to more cut corners, and so on.

Option 3: Implement Change Management

The third option is to add a change-management process that would help management to negotiate a deferral of product features, to slip schedules, and to prioritize fixes to keep the workload level. Figure 5 shows how change management will affect the system.

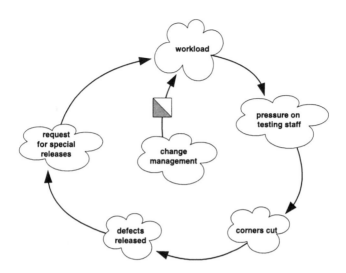

Figure 5. Management responds to the request for a special release by implementing a change management process: Management negotiates with marketing (or customers, if they are internal) to defer features or slip the ship date for the scheduled release. This maintains the current workload, which keeps the system from spinning out of control and buys some time to address underlying quality problems. The shaded square indicates a management action with choice.

This correction won't solve all the problems, but it will probably keep the system from completely breaking down. When you impose a change-management system, you give yourself some breathing room to address other causes at the root of the quality problem.

Risk Consciousness

Once you have one of these options in mind, you'll need time to temper your optimism. By thinking through the downside, you may find a weakness in your idea, or you may be able to develop contingencies. Either way, your solution will emerge with a better chance of success. There's a technical term for this activity: *risk management*.

Assuming you chose to put a change-management process in place, what could go wrong?

- Customers may refuse to negotiate either on priorities or schedules.
- Senior management may agree to implement a change-management process but then back down under pressure from customers.
- Customers may scrap such a defect-ridden product before you get a chance to bring things under control.
- Customers may contact programmers directly and influence them to add fixes or features that were deferred or listed as low priority during the change-management negotiation, leaving testers with the choice of testing the changes (with increased workload) or letting them ship untested (with more defects).

Using this list, you can prepare a backup plan, pay extra attention to getting buy-in from senior management, or choose a different correction.

At this point, having weighed the options and the risks, you are ready to try your change. Keep your diagram of effects and track the results. You are bound to discover factors that you did not consider. Your best defense is to model the system again and to choose the *smallest* correction that will achieve the desired results. With each model and action, you will become better at observing and tempering your action to the system.

Although you may often be tempted to take a dramatic action to correct a problem—especially if customers or senior management are pressing for quick results—you'll find that a major action can lead to a major reaction in a system. The reaction seldom takes you in a direction you want to go, and may make the situation much worse. By practicing this organizational change technique, you can become better at reading system dynamics and choosing the smallest possible correction.

What if senior management demands big action? You still have choices. Model them, build contingencies, and track your results. Just remember that acting decisively doesn't necessarily mean making a drastic correction.

References

Dorner, Dietrich. *The Logic of Failure: Recognizing and Avoiding Error in Complex Situations.* Reading, Mass.: Addison-Wesley, 1996.

The Logic of Failure examines a series of experiments on how people make decisions and take action in complex situations. The results shed light on the way people approach problems and how it can lead to disaster, step by small step.

Hanna, David P. *Designing Organizations for High Performance.* Reading, Mass.: Addison-Wesley, 1988.

Provides an overview of the basic components of organizational design, and provides strategies for implementing change in large organizations.

Schmaltz, David, "Why?" *Compass,* Vol. 3, No. 1 (Spring 1999), pp. 1-2.

A short article that explains different types of causation and how it can affect the way managers think about projects.

Weinberg, Gerald M. *Quality Software Management, Vol. 1: Systems Thinking.* New York: Dorset House Publishing, 1992.

This book is packed with useful ways to think about quality, problems, and software organizations. It introduces the cybernetic model of systems and provides lots of examples and detail about the diagram of effects model discussed in this essay.

How to Create a Process for Developing Useful Scientific Software

Patricia Medvick

S oftware has become an integral component of most scientific research. In many scientific fields, software support has actually become the major portion of the research effort. But software development associated with such scientific endeavors provides few examples of process excellence or even process adequacy. In many small research projects, a single scientist creates custom software for a one-time use. On research teams for larger-scale scientific research—such as those listed later in this essay—the scientists may recognize a need for general use of their software, but generally they remain unaware of software engineering methods and principles.

Scientists are trained in the scientific paradigm, which differs substantially from the engineering paradigm in several ways. Scientists explore by developing or expanding a theory and design experiments to test the "null" hypothesis, but engineers explore risks to achieve a goal while limiting possibilities to acceptable results. Scientists observe by noting what is, perhaps to figure out why it is; but engineers are more active, trying to build things to achieve a goal. The scientists' theory-building and observation techniques do not provide easy stepping-stones to good engineering practice built on goals, risk analysis, and reliable results. The development of scientific software introduces a real engineering world within the scientist's laboratory world.

Beyond the difference in paradigms, the individual attitudes of scientists create further difficulties. Some scientists, for example, are parochial in their views and arrogant about their specialties. They're not likely to honor other disciplines such as software engineering.

Moreover, scientific training does not stress the merits of teamwork or the value of a diverse team for solving problems, and this lack of awareness creates another major hindrance to the development of scientific software that is more useful.

I've seen the struggle between the paradigms and attitudes of science and engineering in many scientific applications of software:

1. **Control of Hardware in Automated Systems.** Here, software is required for controlling hardware in automated systems and dealing with the resulting data. Data handling includes initial gathering, verification, storage, and analysis. Currently, laboratories supporting the human genome effort and pharmaceutical drug discovery are tackling these tasks.

2. **Simulations to Develop Models of Complex Systems.** Massive efforts are devoted to simulations such as those created for exploring traffic pattern components, replicating oceanic and atmospheric systems, and mimicking explosions. Simulations require data gathering, handling, and analysis, along with the software that actually runs the simulation.

3. **Data Mining in Massive Data Sets.** For many sociological and geographic information studies, data mining of data sets is important. This software may be developed for sociological fields as diverse as epidemi-

ology and fraud-and-abuse detection. Software used for geographic image analysis has become increasingly important for environmental explorations.

There is no shortage of standardized software engineering processes designed for a variety of development environments. Numerous books and training courses promote methods that could help establish these processes in a scientific laboratory, yet I've rarely found such processes used in such an environment. In fact, I've met few scientists who were aware of these process models. I have, however, found scientists working on NASA projects and in FDA-regulated drug-testing laboratories who represent notable exceptions to this observation.

If scientists don't use these models, how do they develop software? The most common pattern I've observed is that software is produced under the following assumptions: It will never be modified; it can be used forever; it doesn't need to be tested; and nothing can possibly go wrong. By implication, the scientists seem to say, "I'm not producing software—I'm producing a Law of Nature!"

On small projects, this attitude manifests itself as one scientist, working alone, who creates the software in an ad hoc manner. On larger projects, a single scientist often directs the efforts of a group of software professionals. For example, when the scientist in charge of developing a large simulation lacks software engineering knowledge, the software team can become trapped in a random process that, under deadline pressure, evolves into hero-style software creation.

Heroism in software, however, doesn't scale very well. As software complexity continues to grow, scientific projects need software that is even more reliable. In order to produce and maintain such complex, reliable scientific software, we need well-managed teams of software engineers, not bigger heroes. Consequently, scientific success will depend on maturing the software process.

Moreover, contrary to the "Law of Nature" view some scientist programmers adopt, real research and development require software that can be changed rapidly and accurately. Such an environment places further emphasis on a refined software process.

Then, too, as large projects become interdisciplinary, the language specializations of the different sciences create a Babel-like community. Barriers to communication further inhibit the refinement of a successful software process.

In spite of all these negative factors, several successful approaches to this problem have emerged, and I have witnessed and participated in the production of software products that function well and are maintainable in the scientific environment. These approaches fall into three easily recognized styles:

1. starting small and building incrementally
2. buffering the software process from mismanagement
3. managing well by applying personal standards of excellence

Let's examine each of these success patterns in turn.

Starting Small and Building Incrementally

Initially, when a start-up study's software effort consists of one or two people, maintenance of good communication with the scientific team is a prime prerequisite. Requirements and an expandable design further aid success. Development and maintenance of testing routines guard against unintended side-effects of software changes and help to buffer against the need to rework testing with the addition of each new scientist team member.

Buffering the Software Process from Mismanagement

Projects that start small and build organically usually escape the notice of management until it's too late for management to do much harm to their software engineering practices. However, in massively funded studies, the scientifically trained manager may be more salesperson than engineer. In such a case, the project may be subjected to one of a variety of different styles of mismanagement, with the extremes ranging from micro-mismanagement to macro-nonmanagement. The micro-managing scientist thoroughly enjoys "designing" software and making software architecture decisions. The macro-manager throws the money over the wall and disappears, only to reappear at some random point in the future, demanding results.

Micro-managers frequently direct the development of a so-called prototype that magically becomes the final product—usually during the crisis that follows the termination of funding. Under micro-management, a software team can increase the probability of success by establishing a buffer between the manager and its day-to-day activities. But this isn't easy, because the micro-manager wants to control everything, trusting no one else's judgment or capabilities.

One process for building the buffer starts when a team member gains some level of the micro-manager's trust. Then, when the total lack of progress becomes evident to the project's funding agency, the micro-manager becomes desperate enough to allow the trusted team member to serve as a buffer from responsibility for the software. Once this buffer is in place, the knowledgeable software people can establish a process that fits the requirements of the task at hand.

After wresting control from a micro-manager, the team will find that the most useful process components are version control and reviews of requirements, design, code, and testing procedures. Maintaining communication between team members and defining clear interfaces between modules are also essential for the project to recoup time lost under a micro-manager. The most challenging part of this transformation tends to be requirements gathering, since the scientific manager may not have had a clue about software requirements, yet may have hindered access to customers.

Under a macro-manager, the team should first create a team liaison to the customers. This person's function is primarily to develop, maintain, and guard the growing requirements, which are being developed and modified as the scientists discover new possibilities. The liaison should also develop a timeline by tracking external events, such as project reviews and demonstrations to funding agencies. Another task is to prevent unpleasant surprises, creating communication channels among all participants and calling frequent meetings for development discussions. Presentations featuring early working versions of the final system generate meaningful feedback for further development.

Managing Well by Applying Personal Standards of Excellence

Not all scientifically trained managers are mismanagers. Some do become immersed in software process and produce examples of software excellence. I am personally familiar with two such well-informed managers, each of whom coordinated teams that produced a flexible framework for software simulations. These simulations make use of the massively parallel architectures now available for efforts in the forefront of scientific achievement.

Having learned from many examples of poor process, some scientists search the software engineering literature and have enough respect and patience to implement the diverse processes for building and maintaining good software. The extraordinary teams formed by these scientist engineers live by their personal standards of excellence and make these processes a reality. They gather and analyze requirements and risks. They create a full software design—a design that they review and implement. They maintain a testing suite and documentation for the entire system. Whatever good software process dictates, they do.

What Are the Basics?

In summary, then, what if anything do these approaches to the development of scientific software have in common?

In every example I've seen, there are some absolutely necessary components that may seem easy to establish but are not. There's also a rough order to establishing these components, as follows:

Create a safe environment. Successful project leaders invariably create a safe environment for software developers to practice good processes. This task can be exceptionally difficult for the scientifically trained manager. In many cases, the people who are drawn to the sciences have underdeveloped people skills, and software engineers tend to have similar deficiencies. Without some injection of people skills, a project is doomed to such symptoms of dysfunction as constant screaming at meetings, sulking over lost arguments, obliviousness to communication failures, and efforts to undermine standardization.

Acknowledge human reality. Although scientists themselves are as diverse as their research, I have always found that successful science software project teams somehow establish an appropriate relationship with the scientist who is leading the project, whatever his or her idiosyncratic style might be. In other words, the project is constructed out of real human beings, not stereotypes.

Establish version control. In all successful cases, the initial step of version control is a bottom-line necessity. This is the easiest step to understand, but is neither the most glamorous nor the easiest to implement successfully. Projects that try to accelerate by skipping this step can't go where they want to because they don't know where they are.

Maintain a suitable requirements process. Though they may go about it in different ways, the managers of successful projects establish a requirements process that maintains the quality of the requirements through ongoing communication with customers. Without active and ongoing concentration on communications processes, the project is inevitably strangled by the different languages of the diverse technical specialties and the very different discipline paradigms of the scientists and engineers involved.

Develop a testing mentality. Valid and up-to-date requirements serve as the best foundation for testing, in all of its various forms. Successful projects all use some style of peer review, though seldom anything as formal as is found in the software engineering literature. Peer reviewing represents an integral part of the entire testing process—and on successful projects, this review process gets more than lip service. For example, customized testing routines are developed and kept up-to-date, not shortchanged when the schedule crunch arrives. Successful teams understand that testing is an essential part of the scientific method, a method that applies equally to requirements, design, code, and testing procedures themselves.

Practice architectural discipline. Because scientific research tends to be unpredictable and unplannable, only software designs that are expandable will succeed—not those that are patchable, riggable, and scroungeable. The only teams that succeed are those that work to preserve and update their system architecture, resisting the temptation to patch, rig, and scrounge. In successful projects, I invariably find evidence of architectural discipline in such things as clear inter-module interfaces, regardless of how many times the software has been changed.

Avoid phony demonstrations. The architecture of successful systems is always a *real* architecture. That means that early working versions of the systems provide meaningful feedback for later versions. Many projects fail after developers use showy-but-shallow mock-ups to attract a generous investment from a funding agency, only to see the funding dry up when the phony architecture fails to scale appropriately.

Stay aware of what's real. People on successful projects don't succumb to fantasies of what should be happening. They track external events, such as project reviews and demonstrations to funding agencies. They prevent unpleasant surprises by creating communication channels among all participants. They hold frequent, well-led development discussions in which they validate progress or acknowledge difficulties. They establish processes based on the actual requirements of the task at hand, not on some theory propounded by an outside agency or a textbook.

Scientists must struggle to adopt and respect the theories and practices of software engineering as their dependence on software increases in the coming years. The ability to think like an engineer is becoming a crucial skill for the thinking scientist.

Good Practice Hunting

James Bach

magine that the owner of a trucking company seeks a set of best practices. He hires a driving consultant, and the following conversation ensues:

Client: "I want my drivers to drive at the right speed. In your expert opinion, what is the right speed?"

Consultant: "Hmm. I can't give you a specific number. It depends on a lot of factors."

Client: "Surely, there's a speed that most good drivers generally drive. I don't need abstract driving theory, I just want to know what's the best practice out there."

Consultant: "Good drivers tailor their speed to the situation. There isn't any one speed that's best."

Client: "Oh, obviously we must hire good drivers. That goes without saying. All I really need from you is to tell me what our standard speed should be, based on what the best drivers do. Then our drivers will either use that speed or propose an alternative, as long as they justify their plan and follow it. We're ISO 9000 registered, you know."

Consultant: "The driving process requires different speeds at different times. Any given drive may involve speeds of zero to seventy miles per hour. You can't know the speeds in advance, except very generally. The driver must make a situational judgment."

Client: "Wow, that sounds like it's up to the creativity of individual drivers. How will we get to Level Two on the Driving Maturity Model? I don't need a consultant who says, 'it depends' and offers loosey-goosey guidelines; I need a concrete practice. Capers Jones gives concrete advice and hard numbers—why can't you?"

I know—this is a silly conversation. It's downright ridiculous. No one who knows anything about driving would ever seek to settle on a single, standard "best speed." Yet, in every essential respect, isn't this dialogue typical of the way most of us, most of the time, talk about "best practices"? We look for the one right answer, rather than considering the context. This includes me, too. Just yesterday, I caught myself, mid-sentence, arguing that a certain practice was "bad," even though I had not considered the context in which it was suggested. It's a seductive habit, and one worth kicking.

The goodness of a practice is not an intrinsic attribute. Goodness emerges from the conjunction of a practice and its particular context. I find it useful to think of that context in terms of capability, intent, and situation. Capability is how able we are to do what needs to be done. Intent is our relationship with a mission or goal. Situation is a catchall concept that represents the current state of the world around us as it relates to our practice.

The dialogue on truck-speed methodology seems ridiculous because the roles of capability, intent, and situation are almost too obvious for debate: A competent, licensed driver will choose a reasonable speed; the intent is to deliver goods quickly, without crashing or getting a ticket; situational factors that influence the choice of speed are commonly understood. Capability, intent, and situation are not nearly as clear in the case of software methodology. In software development, it's more difficult to determine the right course of action, and because it's more difficult, we are even more desperate to believe in intrinsically good or bad practices. We want something to give us direction.

The problem of understanding the goodness of our practices is common to us all. But since testing is my business, I'll examine it from that perspective.

Mythologies of Testing

Unfortunately, we aren't very good at observing and evaluating practices. Determining good practice is more often a process of mythology, not engineering or science. By that, I mean our analysis of practice is generally unsystematic, anecdotal, biased, history-bound, personality-driven, vague, exaggerated, and otherwise invites poetic license. Moreover, we generally don't question our myths, passed down as they are from elders and experts, even when they are disseminated outside of the context in which they were originally conceived and blessed.

Part of the problem is that it's difficult to know what practices we're actually using. Does your organization perform unit testing? Are you sure? Unit testing is almost universally recommended and, according to more than one textbook on my bookshelf, is almost universally practiced. In my experience, though, very few companies perform unit testing, and in those that do, I've seen a wide variation in the practice from developer to developer.

Part of this apparent paradox is rooted in the definition of the term. Unit testing, as I understand it, is defined as the testing of individual modules, functions, or classes without regard to their integration with the rest of the system, where the goals of unit testing are to find problems before integration and to find those problems that are difficult to isolate on a subsystem or system level.

The thing is, I've found that this definition is not the one in popular use. Unit testing more often refers to any test activity performed by a developer in the course of development—and most developers have no training or passion for testing. A minor hobby of mine is to ask developers what they do when they unit test. The typical answer is some variation of, "I exercise the code and see if it works." I've discovered that this could mean anything up to and including, "I don't do anything in particular."

The difference between the talk and the actual walk can be startling. I call it the *methodology gap*. Unit testing stands out as a particularly stark example, but I find such gaps, to one degree or another, everywhere I look in typical software projects. Anyone who simply asks practitioners if they're using best practices is likely to get a mythological and inaccurate picture of the practices they actually use.

Another part of the problem of determining best practices is that we don't have very good theoretical models of software engineering. Software engineering is generally treated as an efficient process for creating software that correctly and dependably fulfills a specification. Testing, in that worldview, is a process of generating the smallest set of tests that will reveal discrepancies between the software and its specification. That is certainly an interesting theoretical basis for testing, but it has not proven very helpful for the overwhelming majority of all the testing we do in this industry.

Other branches of science offer models that might put our mythology on better ground. Economics, game theory, and decision theory offer insight into making trade-off decisions.

Principles of cognitive psychology and epistemology could help us understand how testers learn about and evaluate what they test. General systems theory offers ways to decompose and analyze the behavior of complex systems.

As a consequence of practicing software engineering using incomplete theories and inadequate information, we as an industry have adopted wisdom about testing that is at best misleading and at worst damaging:

It's important to repeat the same tests on each new build.

Not necessarily. This practice usually arises when we suspect that a problem introduced into a product could have been detected by an old test but wasn't because we failed to rerun the old test. My experience, however, shows—*Caution: This, too, is mythology*—that this problem is usually far smaller than that of missing defects that were in the product all along while the testers were too busy rerunning old tests and not creating enough new and different tests.

It's important to document all test cases and procedures.

Maybe, but maybe not. Documenting test cases and procedures has at least two negative effects: (1) It tends to result in less overall testing, because of the time required to create and maintain documentation; and (2) it tends to limit the variety of testing, because after documenting the tests, the testers tend to feel obligated to execute only those tests. In the absence of a pressing need for external accountability or a pressing need to share exact test cases with lots of other people, it is probably better when they do not document specific tests. When you test, document just enough to remind you to cover what you need to cover and to report what you need to report.

It's important for testing to be involved early in the test cycle.

That might be a complete waste of time. Most testers want to be involved early in the cycle, but few know what to do when they find themselves there. I can think of a lot of things to do early in a test project, but they require the skills of a technically savvy senior tester or test manager. An unsophisticated or indiscreet tester will only alienate the development staff.

It's important to create tests based on specifications well before it's time to execute them.

Not so fast. Specifications are notoriously and almost universally inadequate for the generation of actual tests. Attempts to use specifications as the basis for test generation usually yield a lot of useless documentation. An examination of specifications for testability and a consultation with developers about improving testability are certainly useful efforts, but such reviews require unusual skill. Reporting defects found in the specification may be useful, too, but doing so requires unusual rapport and diplomacy.

Each of these commonly suggested practices is good to do—in certain situations, when you intend to accomplish certain goals and you have a staff capable of performing them. They are not, however, *intrinsically* good practices.

I'm not against mythology. The kind of research that might provide a comprehensive, scientific foundation for a methodology is expensive and, for the most part, infeasible. So, we're stuck with mythology—and this essay adds to the mythology—but let's admit it before our projects suffer from it.

Practice Cultures

My concerns about practices, their situational goodness and the difficulty of observing them, strike many practical people as academic, and that's understandable. The fact is that we can think of many software development practices that most of us will agree are generally good or generally bad. Some companies have reported tremendous success with the good ones.

Yet once we get past the mythologies and analyze what seems intrinsically good or bad about a practice, we encounter the assumptions about capability, intent, and situation that I mentioned earlier. Though we may not be aware of those assumptions, they can serve as a foundation for evaluating and evolving practices as if they were stand-alone entities. Within a community of people who have a bedrock of shared assumptions (something I call a *practice culture)*, it is indeed meaningful to say that one practice is good and another is bad. "Most of us" agree because we belong to the same community and we aren't even in dialogue with practitioners in other communities.

What made it possible for other fields of engineering to produce handbooks of standards and certification tests for engineers is that each domain of traditional engineering represents a sufficiently cohesive community of practice that has evolved into a theoretical and technological foundation to support the evaluation of its practices. These communities can reasonably account for the variables of situation, intent, and capability. The problem for the software industry is that we consist of umpteen overlapping and fragmented communities, yet our discussions of practice don't account for those communities. In the testing world, for example, I see at least the following broad communities of practice:

Regulated: obligated to prove compliance with external standards

High reliability: spares no effort or expense to produce a highly dependable product

Academic: explores theory at the expense of practical applicability

Contract-driven: obligated to fulfill a specific contract with a specific customer

Market-driven: aims to fulfill a general market need in a competitive environment

Embedded: provides software only as an adjunct to a hardware system

IS: provides business-critical technology for internal users

Cutting across these testing communities are others that are specific to application domains (such as medical information systems, process-control systems, or desktop business applications) or those that are specific to particular technologies (such as relational databases, Internet, or Java).

We're All Methodologists

If testing practices are based on mythology, and that mythology varies from community to community, where does that leave us? We're left to our own devices, more or less. To the extent that we pursue excellence as testers and test managers, each of us must become our own methodologist. To truly and demonstrably perform testing with excellence, you must take control and ownership of testing mythology.

Focusing on methodology means observing and puzzling over the forces that influence how we do our work. It means struggling to articulate models, methods, and heuristics that help us grasp and communicate the essence of the testing craft. One humble and helpful tool I can offer is the following list of questions. Before I adopt a testing practice—for example, using a new test-plan template or test tool—I walk through this list:

1. What objectives are served by this practice? What pain will it relieve?
2. Are those important objectives? Important to whom?
3. In what way are those objectives already served by some other means?
4. What would a highly successful implementation of this practice be worth?
5. How much energy will be required to make it happen? Is there a simpler, cheaper solution?
6. What are the prerequisites for adopting this practice (for example, special training, methods, or tools)?
7. How will this practice disturb or interact with existing practices or processes?

8. What problems or risks will this practice create?
9. How will we know that the practice is helping? How will we assure its quality?
10. If it isn't helping, what will we do then?
11. How much of this practice will be enough, or too much? Can a little of it make a big impact?
12. What alternatives are there to this practice? What if we do nothing?
13. What simple, achievable, self-contained step can be taken toward the new practice?

I once had a brief argument with my friend and colleague Johanna Rothman on the subject of doing regression testing on specific defects that had already been fixed. She thought it was very important to recheck fixed bugs on a regular basis; I thought it was a waste of time.

After some discussion about this, I rolled out some data to prove my point—*Mythology alert: My data came from a single project and had been collected several years earlier*—and I told her that on a population of 2,000 defects fixed over a six-month period, I had measured only a 2 percent recurrence rate. But wait! Johanna revealed data of her own that showed a recurrence of 40 percent!

Hearing about her data, I felt incredulous for a moment, then almost said, "You're crazy, Johanna. That number has got to be wrong." But I didn't say it. Another, wiser thought popped up, and I asked instead, "Johanna, how can we account for the difference in our data?"

Well, we worked it out, and sure enough, I finally had to admit that, for her particular technology, rechecking certain classes of old defects should be an essential part of the test strategy. Situational practice wins again.

That's the thought I want to leave you with. The next time you feel the urge to pass ultimate judgment on the goodness or badness of a testing practice, pause a moment. It all depends.

Epilogue

Naomi Karten

I f your organization is one in which confusion and chaos are unfamiliar states, feel free to skip these final thoughts. Otherwise . . . When things go awry, as they inevitably do, we human beings are often quick to find fault with others. This is putting the They Syndrome to work ("They should have . . ." and "Why didn't they . . . ?"). Being the competent people we are, we need barely a nanosecond to locate the source of responsibility elsewhere. Our challenge is to remember to stop and ask, How might I have contributed to this situation? What might I have done to prevent it? What can I do to avoid a recurrence?

As the essays in this collection illustrate, improvements in effectiveness can be made at the team and organizational level, as well as at the personal level. But, tempting though it may be to try to fix what's out there ("If only they would . . ."), we're more likely to enhance effectiveness if we start by looking within and asking ourselves what we might do better or differently.

To emphasize the words of Virginia Satir, "Change happens one person at a time." That person is you, me, each of us.

The goal of this book's seventeen contributors has been to share with you some of the lessons we've learned as we've worked to amplify our own effectiveness. Rest assured that we, like you, make mistakes, fall into familiar traps, forget the lessons we should have learned by now, and from time to time, make a muddled mess of things.

Happily, we've learned we can always get better at acknowledging our snafus, listening to the wisdom of others (even if it doesn't always sound like wisdom at the time), and learning from our experiences. Our hope is that from this book, you too will find a few ideas to help you improve your own effectiveness and, in doing so, to help others improve theirs. Happy unmuddling, and please stay in touch.

Contributors

James Bach   james@satisfice.com • www.satisfice.com

James Bach is founder and principal consultant of Satisfice, Inc. James cut his teeth as a programmer, tester, and SQA manager in Silicon Valley and the world of market-driven software development. He has worked at Apple, Borland, a couple of start-ups, and some consulting companies, including a stint as chief scientist at STLabs, an independent software testing laboratory. He was part of the team that defined the body of knowledge covered by the Certified Software Quality Engineer program for the American Society for Quality, and has served on curriculum advisory boards for the Rochester Institute of Technology and the International Technological University.

Through his articles and seminars on good enough quality, exploratory testing, and heuristic test design, James helps individual software testers think clearly about testing, cope with complex projects, and answer the questions, "What am I doing here?" and "What should I do now?" Find James Bach's articles and models on-line at his Website.

Marie Benesh   mbenesh@omegapt.com • www.omegapt.com

Marie Benesh is a principal consultant with Omega Point Consulting, an IT management consulting firm. She has led an infrastructure implementation of PeopleSoft, and she consults to both Fortune 500 organizations and universities on ERP implementation, IT management practices, and organizational change efforts.

Rick Brenner   rbrenner@ChacoCanyon.com • www.ChacoCanyon.com

Rick Brenner is principal of Chaco Canyon Consulting. He works with technology and software organizations that want to make complex products and need state-of-the-art teamwork, and with organizations that want to create innovative products by building stronger relationships between their people. In his twenty years as a software developer, software development manager, entrepreneur, and consultant, he has developed valuable insights into the interactions between people in a technical environment, and between people and the technological media in which they work.

Rick holds a Master's degree in Electrical Engineering from MIT. His current interests focus on improving personal and organizational effectiveness in abnormal situations, as in the case of dramatic change, technical emergencies, and high-pressure project situations. His numerous essays on these subjects are available at his Website.

Esther Derby   derby@estherderby.com • www.estherderby.com

Esther Derby has more than twenty years' experience in software development. She's been a programmer, systems manager, project manager, and internal consultant. She currently runs her own consulting firm, Esther Derby Associates, Inc., based in Minneapolis. Esther works with people to increase their effectiveness in understanding and managing complex systems, such as software development organizations and software development projects.

Kevin Fjelsted   kfjelsted@pcte.com • www.pcte.com

Kevin Fjelsted founded K & M Development Consultants in 1994 to help business owners and senior managers meet the challenges of today's constantly changing technology. Under the aegis of K & M, Kevin provides a wide range of computer consulting services, assisting managers in understanding the role of technology in their particular business, incorporating what they need for the future into what they already have, and helping them to migrate to new technologies that can improve their efficiency and better serve their clients. Then, as a strategic systems architect, Kevin puts it all together, ensuring that the new system and software work exactly as planned.

For the past twenty years, Kevin's work has been on the cutting edge of systems and software development. His background includes nine years in executive management as well as solid experience in all aspects of product development: specification, estimating, programming, testing, consulting, installation, and budgeting.

This breadth of experience allows him to bring a unique perspective as well as an unmatched level of expertise to each project. Perhaps the most important point about Kevin's background is simply this: His entire career has been focused on implementing solutions that meet the customer's needs and requirements.

Don Gray   don@SystemsSmiths.com • www.SystemsSmiths.com

Don Gray works with manufacturers in evaluating, establishing, and executing their automation plans. This work involves everything from sensors to production and process data. Don has been working as an independent consultant since 1984. He enjoys solving problems and working with people, and currently he's working on a better understanding of how people interact in solving complex technical problems. Don brings a unique perspective on life to his writing—having produced such articles as "How to Kill a Company"—and to his teaching, having taught general computing (both software and hardware) and application-specific classes.

Naomi Karten   nkarten@compuserve.com • www.nkarten.com

Naomi Karten is a student of human behavior. She has presented seminars and keynotes to more than 100,000 people internationally on how to manage customer expectations, close communication gaps, and build trusting, supportive relationships. She is also an instructor for the Weinberg and Weinberg workshop, Problem Solving Leadership (PSL).

Naomi is the author of several books, including *Managing Expections: Working with People Who Want More, Better, Faster, Sooner, NOW!* and *How to Establish Service Level Agreements.* Readers have described her newsletter, *Perceptions & Realities,* as lively, informative, and a breath of fresh air.

Before forming her business in 1984, Naomi earned a B.A. and an M.A. in Psychology, and gained extensive experience in technical, customer support, and management positions. Her Website is regularly updated with articles on topics such as managing expectations, gathering client feedback, relationship building, and developing service savvy.

Bob King   bob@rc-king.com • www.rc-king.com

Bob King consults with project teams when they are beginning—and beginning again. He helps project teams to see how things fit together and what work is required to assemble them. He mentors team members in how to gather requirements and how to envision and document the architecture of applications. His goal is to work himself out of a job in every project.

Before forming his consulting practice in 1996, Bob worked his way up and out of the technical career path at American Express Financial Advisors. During his sixteen years there, he helped start up a subsidiary in England as an expatriate, design and develop their mission-critical financial planning application, and plan and architect their initial on-line banking efforts. Bob has a B.A. in Mathematics and an M.S. in Computer Science.

Pat Medvick   Patricia.Medvick@pnl.gov

Pat Medvick was a software engineer with Los Alamos National Laboratory for fifteen years and president of Coyote Software for two years. She recently joined the staff at Pacific Northwest National Laboratory. Prior to obtaining her M.S. in Computer Science, she utilized her B.S. in Biology and Ph.D. in Oceanography as an environmental biologist. Since 1985, she has worked on automation for the Human Genome project, database design for the GenBank project, magnetoencephalography data analysis, software improvement of an automated system for pharmaceutical high-throughput screening, and numerous simulation projects. With her experience as an application developer, software designer, and project lead, Pat has the abilities to jell software teams and to guide software process improvement in a research and development environment.

Brian Pioreck
BPioreck@aol.com

Brian Pioreck first fell in love with computers in 1978 while studying for a career in ornamental horticulture. With just nine credits left to complete his degree in the subject, he followed his heart and dropped out of school to pursue computer work. He taught himself to program on a Vic-20, and with the help of night school and vigorous self-study, he found himself in the business of growing technology and technical teams instead of growing flowers.

Brian has held various positions in software development, technical management, and management consulting over the last seventeen years. Currently, he concentrates on raising the awareness of human systems in organizations and of methods to improve performance. Brian currently helps development organizations hit their market window with a balanced combination of features, performance, and quality.

Sharon Marsh Roberts
Ken Roberts
Sharon@Roberts-1.com
Ken@Roberts-1.com

Sharon Marsh Roberts and Ken Roberts work with large corporations on projects that are new to the corporations—on implementations their clients would prefer to avoid. They also write together, and for fun, they are active in backcountry skiing and tandem bicycling.

Both Sharon and Ken use their business and technical expertise to facilitate multidisciplinary teams, bringing together technical experts and business leaders to tackle new and difficult projects. Ken has worked primarily with companies in the insurance and pharmaceutical industries. Sharon has worked in financial reporting and systems for companies in entertainment, banking, insurance, and pharmaceuticals.

Ken is a Fellow in the Society of Actuaries and has a Ph.D. in Computer Science. Sharon is a C.P.A. with an M.B.A. and an Advanced Professional Certificate in Finance and Accounting. Sharon has served as chair of the Independent Computer Consultants Association (ICCA), in which capacity her goal was to seek new ways for consultants to work together to meet the needs of their clients.

Ken has authored ten scientific papers, and his Ph.D. thesis was on active touch with a multi-finger robot hand. At AT&T Bell Labs, he researched computer vision and animation. He has also consulted with clients on major issues, ranging from interest-rate derivatives to business process risk analysis and contingency planning. Ken has designed and programmed innovative systems and has managed multi-person teams. Most recently, he led an international life insurance project for a major insurance company.

Sharon's projects have included systems to implement executive and technical leaders' compensation plans, an FDA-mandated system to identify and collect nonclinical payments to investigators on clinical studies, an insurance system to pay physicians in managed-care arrangements, and numerous financial reporting systems.

Johanna Rothman   jr@jrothman.com • www.jrothman.com

Johanna Rothman observes and consults on managing high-technology product development. She works with her clients to find the leverage points that will increase their effectiveness as organizations and as managers, helping them ship the right product at the right time and recruit and retain the best people.

Johanna publishes *Reflections,* an acclaimed quarterly newsletter about managing product development. Johanna's handbook, *Hiring Technical People: A Guide to Hiring the Right People for the Job*—forthcoming in a new edition from Dorset House Publishing—has proved a boon to perplexed managers, as have her articles in *Software Development, Cutter IT, IEEE Computer, Software Testing & Quality Engineering,* and *IEEE Software.*

Johanna is the founder and principal of Rothman Consulting Group, Inc., and is a member of the clinical faculty of The Gordon Institute at Tufts University, a practical management degree program for engineers.

Steven M. Smith

steve@stevenmsmith.com • www.stevenmsmith.com

Steve Smith works at the intersection of people, management, and systems, helping organizations to become more productive.

Although most of Steve's career has been technical—starting in 1975 as a systems programmer—over the years, his context has widened. Today, he tackles the most difficult problem businesses face: managing technical people so they achieve results rather than merely justifying and deploying the latest technology.

Steve is a consultant, author, speaker, and expert facilitator and coach who honors and enhances the wisdom that lies dormant in groups. He works as a systems engineer for EMC, a manufacturer of intelligent storage systems, software, and services.

Contributors

Eileen Strider
EileenStrider@worldnet.att.net • www.striderandcline.com

Eileen Strider consults with people in IT organizations and projects to help them succeed, especially when they are feeling frustrated and stuck. She works with IT and business professionals to determine what is happening and to recommend actions for improving their chances of success. Her consulting engagements range from small in-house projects to large ERP efforts and from a single work group to entire IT organizations. During her thirty years of technical, management, and consulting experience in large IT organizations, she has developed a practical, no-nonsense approach that she brings to her clients' work. Using her experience as CIO of a large insurance corporation, she is highly skilled in communicating to business executives what they must do to support their IT projects and organizations.

Eileen is a partner with Wayne Strider in Strider & Cline, Inc. Their highly successful Leaders' Forum is held annually in Crested Butte, Colorado. She is also an instructor for the Weinberg and Weinberg Problem Solving Leadership Workshop and co-facilitator of Jerry Weinberg's Systems Effectiveness Management Group.

Gerald M. Weinberg
hardpretzel@earthlink.net • www.geraldmweinberg.com

For more than forty years, Jerry Weinberg has worked on transforming software organizations. He is author or co-author of many articles and books, including *The Psychology of Computer Programming: Silver Anniversary Edition*. His books cover all phases of the software life cycle. They include *Exploring Requirements, Rethinking Systems Analysis & Design, Handbook of Walkthroughs, Inspections, and Technical Reviews*, and *General Principles of Systems Design*. His books on leadership include *Becoming a Technical Leader, The Secrets of Consulting*, and the *Quality Software Management* four-volume series.

To many, Jerry is best known for his workshops for software leaders. These include Systems Effectiveness Management (SEM), Problem Solving Leadership (PSL), and the Congruent Organizational Change-Shop.

Becky Winant
rwinant@espritinc.com • www.espritinc.com

Becky Winant broke into software programming in the early 1970's on the advice of a bridge partner. From that point on, she planned to connect her education and passion for art with her growing respect for software and engineering. First, she explored computer graphics, APL, and computer time-sharing. In the early 1980's, she discovered visual software modeling at Yourdon under Tim Lister's management. After managing design and seminar groups at Yourdon, she decided to go it alone in promoting systems analysis and design. In 1985, she cofounded Esprit Systems Consulting with Robert Medrala, serving as president, principal consultant, mentor, and course author.

Esprit has built a first-class reputation in embedded systems methods education and consulting. This comes from advocating team skills with a deep understanding of analysis and design modeling principles. Becky's clients have described her as down-to-earth, practical, and well-informed.

Becky has been a speaker at many conferences and has been published in *Object Magazine, JOOP, Automotive Manufacturing International,* Auerbach's *Software Engineering Magazine,* and Wiley's *Software Engineering Encyclopedia.*

Index